Gently Dented

For TLW
Thank you for the conversations

Introduction

Hello, my name is Meaghan and I live with schizoaffective disorder (bipolar disorder and schizophrenia). This book is part biography and part explanation of my mental disorder. The story of my life is affected by my disorder and my disorder is affected by the story of my life. There are areas where my story is unique and other parts that are commonplace. Hopefully there is enough value in my uniqueness to warrant a book.

I shall state right now that I live in a mental health bubble. Ever since I decided to seek treatment, I've always been able to ensure that there was enough money to pay for my psychiatrist and medication. I have been fortunate that way. I go to therapy on a regular basis. There are those who suffer with a disorder who don't have the means or money for quality care. My story doesn't include homelessness or rehab. It includes a stint in a mental facility, several different medications, and a decades-long struggle to live as normal as a life as possible.

With schizoaffective disorder, it's hard to focus. A lot of people have asked what's the point of this book? The point is a person with schizoaffective disorder sat down and wrote about her disorder. Years of my life are grouped into chapters and the chapters are linear. However, within the chapters it's a free-for-all of events. Putting them together in any other form makes my head want to fall off from spinning. I also happen to be bad at transitions.

There isn't much humor in this book. I tried to inject some into my story as I love a good laugh and am always up for a joke. It's just that as I sat down to write this book, I uncovered something about myself: for me, there is nothing funny about my mental disorder. In all seriousness, when it comes to my mental health and treatment, it's not all fun and games.

Having said that, I will also state that I'm mainly a pleasant person. I take life as it is and try to remain as balanced as possible, no matter how off my brain is being. This pleasantness has served me well in this life. It helps me appear to not be a somewhat raving lunatic to strangers.

Oh, and my memory sucks. All my stories are one sided and told as honestly from my point of view as possible. Throughout the years my brain has taken a lot of beatings. It is important to tell my story with as much truth as possible, so if there was any story that I couldn't quite remember, I didn't tell it. Every story is from my memory and how I see the world. There are always two sides to all interactions, but I only know my side. My side is what is portrayed here. I didn't try to guess other people's interpretations because I would end up an even bigger lunatic if I did.

I shall also add that names have been changed to protect the innocent. I love my friends and some have agreed to let me use their real names. You know, to spice things up a bit.

One of the characteristics of living with schizoaffective is an unstructured mind. There is little logic to be found in my train of thought. One of the key ways I'm explaining my disorder is by leaving my prose in a semi-state of disarray. Here I am asking you, as the reader, to go into this book with an open mind about reading my story. I have a severe mental disorder, so make yourself comfortable, you're about to enter the mind of a bipolar schizophrenic.

Chapter One

Gently Dented

Living with a mental illness is like living in the sea. Not on a boat or an island but actually bobbing up and down out in the middle of the ocean. Most days are spent just out there all by myself with land in the distance. When a storm comes, it's all I can do to not drown and several times I think I will. The fight to stay afloat feels like an insurmountable task. Then without warning, the storm passes and I'm back just being in the calm sea. Spending my days trying to stay afloat in the sea is bad but the storms are worse. Then there are rare days, where land is beneath my feet. Ah, precious land. Is this beautiful wondrous feeling of dry land without a care in my mind how a normal brain feels? Envy is not something that is comfortable living in my heart. However, the moments I'm on land makes me jealous of people who don't have this illness. Land is lovely but an uncomfortable feeling haunts me. How long will this last? A few minutes, a few hours, or if I'm lucky, a few days. Never longer than a few days. Then after the time on dry land ends, it's back to the water, normally with a storm brewing. Fear of knowing I can be yanked off the place most everyone lives fills my heart with terror. Will I be strong enough to fight another storm? Can I handle a life of just bobbing up and down all on my own? Trust me, no one can save me. It's all up to me. No one can reach into my brain and fix me.

Living with a mental illness while taking medicine helps by giving a life raft of support. I'm still out there in the great big sea, but no longer am I stranded needing to use all the strength in my soul to just stay alive. I live with a raft next to me and when a storm comes, medication offers a raft to cling onto to keep me from drowning. Time on land is a little more carefree because of the aid of medication. Time on land also becomes longer. Weeks can go by before the ocean drags me back. Ah, weeks. That's something growing up I never thought I would have. To go weeks without a hiccup in my brain. I can actually feel as though I may never be sick again. While I'm on land the life raft is still near me and I know my day-to-day struggle won't be as hard. All this talk of medication makes it sound like I should've been taking meds all along. However, when I moved out on my own, medication was not something I considered.

The medications on the market in the 1990s were terrible. I had already tried a few and the side effects weren't worth it. I felt strung out all of the time and my eyes would dilate. Those terrible medications from the 1990s made several people think I was high on illegal drugs. I have a paranoia about people thinking I'm doing something I'm not. If I were to be accused of taking drugs illegally, my mind would literally explode, or something worse. Who knows what. My mind won't let me imagine what would be worse than my brain actually exploding. Medications at that time made me foggy and even though they helped reduce the severity of episodes, I couldn't have others thinking I was taking drugs. Why then are medications a life raft? Newer medications are a life saver. The time between being a kid, then a teenager were not fun but in my early 20s I started to find what medications would help me out the best. Until that period of my life started, there I was, trying to not completely give in, without help.

I have a deep-seated fear that everyone hates me and is out to judge me. It has made me judgmental in the sense that I judge people thinking they're judging me. It makes me a little confrontational and standoffish. Not in real life. I'm actually quite nice. The fear, paranoia, and judging all goes on in my head. I kind of don't know how much of it is standard run-of-the-mill thoughts everyone plays out in their minds and how much of it is my disorder. I imagine everyone has this issue a little so I'm not entirely unique in this manner. I accept that. However, I will use terms like "everyone" and "always" instead of "some people" and "sometimes." I've left some of these thoughts intact in this book because I'm trying to illustrate what it's like in my head, whether or not my thought process can be considered common.

My life is ordinary and unusual at the same time. I live in a contradiction. I live with a disorder that contradicts itself. There is so much noise in my head that it can be hard to think straight. I hope by exploring my life and my schizoaffectiveness, I may give voice to the others out there who want to live as normal a life as possible but have an internal struggle every day to just stay afloat in their very own ocean.

Chapter Two

Crazy from the Start

"Bipolar with psychotic tendencies" was my initial diagnosis. I was 16, however, I've had this illness my entire life. "Psychotic tendencies" is almost like schizophrenia-light. There are schizophrenic symptoms but not enough for a full diagnosis. That is what I have lived with my entire life. That is all I know. Yes, medication gives me a helping hand, but I will never know how great it must be to have a normal brain. If you're not living with a mental illness, you have a normal brain. Please take your lovely brain for granted but don't look down on those with a disorder. Just because you don't understand an issue doesn't mean it doesn't exist. The frustration of hearing people who live in willful ignorance judge me led me to hide my disorder as best as I could. Sometimes I would flatly deny my mental situation when it was suspected. I don't want feelings of contempt or the opposite in the form of saccharine sympathy. I want understanding and kindness. I live with a disorder that can't be seen physically. I may be walking down the street freaking out because in my mind there are flesh-eating bugs on my skin and my medication is at home, but all one will see is a lady briskly walking who looks like she has a terrible itch.

This is something that has corrupted my behavior but it's not part of my soul. To know the difference in a mentally ill person is important.

The worry that the psychotic tendencies would lead to something else was a huge fear. Fear that my illness would evolve into something more. My fears became true right around the time I was at the age schizophrenia rears its ugly head to an unsuspecting poor soul. Why was I afraid of developing schizophrenia? Well, there's a family history of the disorder on my dad's side. Then there's the simple fact that all of my life, inanimate objects talked to me. Not only were the ups and downs of bipolar disorder running rampant, I had to deal with forks telling me which one of them wanted to be used. If I picked up a fork that wanted to stay in the drawer, it would scream until I put it down and picked up the one that wanted to be used. There was also a case of paranoia, because why not? Why not have an extra layer of crazy along with the basket of crazy that was preloaded?

I tried not to dwell too much on the possibility of schizophrenia. The signs were hard to ignore and I wasn't convinced I was up for the challenge. Bipolar with psychotic tendencies was already almost too much to handle. How would I live with one step higher? Would I fall into an abyss I couldn't get out of? I just had to shelve those thoughts and deal with life as it came. Schizophrenia was a bridge I would have to cross if I ever came to it. And I did come to it.

When the paranoia is filling my head, I begin to think everyone hates me. I start to believe everyone has a mission to destroy me. Be it bosses, coworkers, friends, acquaintances, or the person behind me in cash register line and my transaction is proving to be a little complicated. I begin to believe everyone, and I mean that in the truest sense if the word, is out to destroy me.

I have always believed that there are those who must smell my disorder, mistake it for weakness, and proceed to make my life hell. To be frank, these interactions of hell on Earth via a person aren't specific to me. It's just hyper-amplified because I'm already paranoid that everyone hates me.

This thought makes it hard to focus and causes mixed episodes to happen. A mixed episode is when I'm both manic and depressed at the same time. Having a mixed episode means I'm hiding in bed wanting to go out and be fun and amazing and spend lots of money but not having the energy or the will to do any of those things. It feels like my brain is being ripped in two.

Mixed episodes and mania are the two types of episodes I experience the most. Depression used to be something I could beat because I knew the depression wasn't real and so even though I didn't want to get out of bed, shower, and brush my teeth I could use that rationale to beat it. Anti-depressants have not been a class of medication I have taken all that often and it has been over a decade since it has been a part of the team of drugs that helps me stay afloat. That is, until recently.

When I'm having a paranoid episode, I see things that aren't there. I can make up negative situations to prove no one likes me. Not only do I think everyone hates me, I think everyone is out to get me. I start believing even my time-tested friends hate me. A few years ago my cousin, Sean, didn't return a text of mine for over a week and I became convinced he never wanted to talk to me again and was taking it one step further: he was badmouthing me to our family. My family and I don't really go out of our way to communicate with each other so their silence should've been expected. I just couldn't talk myself out of the thought process.

Sean did text me back and said he was busy at work and that's why he hadn't responded. Within a moment of reading his words, all was forgiven. I even forgave him for being tied up with his job.

I didn't forgive him to his face though. Never to his face. I don't like to admit to anyone when I'm being paranoid and with the elation of communication came a deep sense of guilt about my train of thought. I keep repeating to myself: the paranoia is fake but the pain is real. The paranoia gets stuck on repeat. I'll stop now and will move on.

I live with several types of episodes. Paranoid and schizophrenic episodes are common place. I've had intense episodes of depression. However, my episodes are usually either manic or mixed. I always know when I'm having a mixed episode. Mania is harder to spot.

Some say the hardest of the seven deadly sins to spot is pride (Okay, I got that from the seven deadly sins episode of Charmed. [S3 Ep18 "Sin Francisco."] I don't watch TV for intellectual stimulation). Pride can mask as normal. Mania can hide as happiness. I honestly don't know how it feels to just be happy and/or content. I am happy for a moment and then full-on complete manic mode the next. Every joyous occasion turns to mania.

How to describe mania? Let me enlighten you. The common description is having racing thoughts, spending money, and doing a bunch of crazy out-of-control shit. It's all true, I tell ya. It's all true. It would be so much fun to ride the wave of mania if it didn't mean another reason my brain has to not be normal.

Racing thoughts is a stupid way to describe the symptom. Alas, it's the only one that fits. Sort of. My thoughts become surprisingly calm and come at a pleasant speed but it's incredibly hard to pin them down and form them into words. If I'm stuttering it's because I'm manic. Most people talk fast when they talk but I tend to talk slower. This is the only way I can hide how my brain is behaving.

I do spend an incredible amount of money. In 2010, my last non-pregnancy related major manic episode, I started charging everything on my credit card. Things that weren't needed. Just things I talked myself into needing. I spent and spent until $2000 had been spent in three weeks. This may not seem like a lot of money to those with money but I worked in retail for fourteen years. That $2000 took me eight weeks to earn. This episode was kept hidden from my husband Jonathan. Stress filled my heart when I looked at my balance. How to break the news to him? Well, by not telling him at all. That was my brilliant strategy. I worked and brought in money. I'll just take six months to pay it off and Jonathan will never know. Well, as the date of payment became closer and closer, I realized I wasn't saving enough to pay off as much as I needed to. Stressed out isn't a strong enough term to describe my state. I actually lost 10 pounds due to being too stressed out to eat. Jonathan decided to check on my credit spending and looked at the statement. He has the passwords to all my financial goings-on. If you're horrified by that fact, well then you're about to learn the lesson as to why that's necessary. Understandably, he freaked out. I tried to explain my plan to pay everything off but that was to no avail and the credit card was turned over to him. This restriction of my spending money has never bothered me. As you can tell, I'm terrible with money.

What is different from how mania is described for me? Two ways. 1) I believe I'm God's favorite person and nothing can stop my greatness and 2) Manic episodes make me burst with orgasmic joy.

Everyone lives their life just fine and never knows they were in the presence of the most blessed person on the planet. God wanted me to change the world for the better. I would make the most human, intuitive films in the history of films. I would be perfect in every aspect. I would produce the best children. I would write the great memoir.

As I've grown older this feeling of being God's chosen one has faded. No longer do I feel like every aspect of my fate is going to change the course of humanity. I'm old enough to be content with my boring life. I have come to accept that I live a boring life but I'm a not boring person. I love to take tea. I read books and watch movies and listen to music, just like everyone else. I love to spend time with my sons. Having a quiet little life is good enough for me.

Having said that, I still walk around knowing that God loves me more than you and to reward me, he's giving me the greatest gift of all, an orgasm just for me. This normally lasts for days. It's a little bit hard to explain this part of a manic episode. Let's face it, it's enormously embarrassing to talk about. Flying high on the greatness of mania also comes with an orgasmic mode. This is why so many manics cheat on their spouse. The sexual feeling that comes with each seriously damaging episode is great. It's hard to come down from this aspect of a manic episode. It's hard, but doable. For a few days I go around in this near climactic state. Sexual energy flows down my arms and through my fingers. It's thrilling and horrifying at the same time. Who wants to do their daily chores, like dishes, laundry, or cleaning when the orgasmic state is nurtured by shopping? At the mall, online, at Target. Anywhere money is taken. It almost becomes too much to function on any sort of level.

Going to work is also a challenge. Who wants to be at work when they are getting orgasms from the divine deity? I walk around knowing that God loves me more than you.

When I'm in the middle of an orgasmic energy manic state, I don't want the episode to end. Like sexual acts, it does end and that's when the shame floods in. I don't go around having sex with strangers but it's embarrassing after the fact to have that particular type of episode. I'm a bit of a prude and normally sex talk leaves me blushing. To have the feeling of sexual energy running through my veins horrifies me. I do understand completely the need to go have one night stands. The prude in me keeps that from happening. Ha ha.

I actually hate manic episodes. The heightened sense of joy and mania make me feel like I'm losing control. I don't like losing control. I just want to be in control of my brain, which is something that is elusive to me. Manic episodes have been described before as being a lot of fun. That level of excitement and ecstasy can be enticing. It may be fun for others with my disorder, but not for me. I actually dread manic episodes. The heightened sense of joy and elation means my disorder is basically one big giant mind control loss. As thrilling as mania is, it just reminds me I'm not always in charge of me.

Abrupt subject change: Psychotic tendencies became hilarious to me from a very early age. I was about eight when I discovered that not everyone hears their stuffed animals actually talk to them. I've always have had moments where it felt as though the air and water is filled with flesh-eating bugs. It isn't normal. I can go up to a week without bathing because the water is attacking me. I'll sleep head to toe under the covers because there are bugs in the air. These scenarios happen often enough but when I'm flesh-eating-bug free, I can take a nice hot shower and sleep without covers. It's hard for me to grasp that this symptom really happens during periods when it's not going on but there it is.

The first "friend" I made was a Christmas dog stuffed animal. His name was Krismutt and he started talking to me the day after he was given to me as a present. If you're wondering what the various voices sound like and where they come from, I'll do my best to explain. As a child I never heard the term "auditory hallucinations." The voices I heard were not in my head but as clear as day. Clear enough to be confident they are talking to me as though I was listening to other people or hearing any outside noise. It's as if I'm talking to you in reality. They're outside my head. Every object had its own voice too. The tomato telling me to throw it out because it was too depressed to become a tasty part of a meal sounded different than the tomato who was telling me it wanted to be cooked. I couldn't cut the sad tomato because it would scream in pain and cry. Sometimes people tell me my auditory hallucinations are like when a tomato they're trying to cut slides around and falls off the cutting board. So much they jokingly say, "This tomato doesn't want to be cooked." If the tomato isn't talking to you with its own voice, then the two scenarios are completely different and please don't compare the two. With the hilarity of inanimate objects talking to me, there's a secret worry that the voices would start to scream until I did some evil deed. I would deal with the issue if it ever arrived. However that hasn't happened and I'm confident it never will. As a child, then a teen and, before I knew it, a young adult, I would laugh when the TV wished me "good morning."

Okay, so Krismutt's storyline is this: He remained one of my best friends until I started taking medication to stop the voices. For the 14 years prior, I couldn't sleep at home without him. If I was at a sleepover or hotel, I sucked it up. I didn't take him out of the house because I'm not dumb. Krismutt knew all of my secrets. He was my own private friend. I was aware his talking voice was not truly real and that it was something my brain conjured up. However, it was nice to have someone to talk to and have them talk back. How did I go about hiding conversations with Krismutt? My voice was in my mind. We talked with telepathy on my part and auditory hallucinations on Krismutt's end.

When his voice was silenced, I mourned his loss, but it was time to let go. Whenever my medications were off, Krismutt would come back and for some reason, each time he would be mean. Every time he was meaner than the time before. I put him in the bottom of my closet, but there he was, stressing me out with all his anger about me silencing him. It got so bad that when I was pregnant with my second child and the voices started back up again, I threw him away. I wonder if I had stayed off the medications in the first place would our friendship still be great? My desire to be well was and still is greater than the desire to have a best friend by means of a stuffed dog.

Whenever I have an episode I can only concentrate a few feet in front of my face. I lower my head and internalize my energies on just being able to walk without slipping into the depths of despair. The real world becomes noise I can't handle. This is one of the main reasons I don't like getting out of bed when suffering from an episode. Watching television becomes too much work. Putting on day clothes

loved the sense of community. Which why it breaks my heart that at a very young age, I discovered I didn't believe in Jesus. I was nine and sitting in Sunday School, where the teacher was talking about Jesus's love, and the epiphany hit me. Jesus wasn't in my heart. Did I believe he existed? Check. Did I believed in Heaven and Hell? Check. Did I believe in God? Double check. Is Jesus is in my heart? Nope. Not even a little. There I was, a mere nine-years-old, having an existential crisis. I prayed every night for two years to die young. All children go to Heaven right? Dying as a child was my only way into Heaven. I didn't die and by the age of eleven, I was forced to come to the conclusion that either Christianity wasn't the only true religion or I was going to Hell. This was something I struggled with throughout my teenage years. I really want to be one of the millions of people who know that Jesus Christ is their personal Lord and Savior but I can't. Everyone is different in their own right and we are all wired differently. Our differences make the world go round and should be celebrated. However, having only one true religion seems bitterly unfair to me. Mental illness or no, I'm simply not wired in a way to believe in a God that would make me so different in my outlook on life and then tell me I had to believe a certain way. I wish I had the passion for religion. I really do. I slightly envy people who have complete faith. It's something I'll never have. Around eighteen, I made peace with the possibility of rotting for an eternity in Hell. I had to be true to myself and live as well as I could. If God feels I need to be punished for that, then so be it.

Lying was a trait both my mother and father taught me. My main lesson from Dad was that lying to his face was the only way I could survive his judgmental presence. Mom told stories and was full of mischief. Telling stories that simply weren't true but nice to imagine are true and pass them off to anyone listening as truth was fun. Both examples of lying helped give me the skills to cover up my illness to the outside world. I knew how to lie to save myself from the judgmental people out there who refuse to understand mental illnesses and Mom's creative style taught me how to make something up as to my whereabouts. Instead of confessing I had been lying in bed for days, I could invent something far more fun. Like seeing a movie by myself (when my episode only needed a day of rest) to being gone for a while on a personal vacation (when I could schedule my work shifts around an episode).

My lying did not come without its downfalls. In sixth grade, I lost my best friend to all the lying. She warned me that she wasn't going to be friends with someone whose words she didn't believe once she figured out how much I was lying. I liked her a lot but lying was integrated into my system. Like oxygen, lying was an intricate part of my existence. The day came when I told one too many falsehoods and she stayed true to her promise. It hurt but it didn't make me learn the valuable lesson of being a truth-teller. It took me until my late teens to stop lying on a regular basis. It just became too old and I was having a hard time keeping my stories straight. It just wasn't worth it anymore.

Kleptomaniac. Stealing started off as a lack of understanding of what money is. Around the age of six, when my mom would take me grocery shopping, I would take packs of gum from the impulse item display. I thought ringing up products was the way inventory was tracked. I knew I was throwing off inventory but I didn't realize the implications of my actions. One day my mom caught me stealing gum. She sat me down and explained what money is and how stealing is bad. Now I knew the concept of money. Armed with this knowledge, I still continued to steal. It was simple, I didn't have money but I wanted things. Who would care if I stole the items I wanted even if it was something that is worse than simply throwing inventory off?

For a brief time, in sixth grade, I was a Girl Scout. Being a Girl Scout was fun but of course, I ruined everything.

The first strike was when I accidentally gave my troop head lice. None of the adults in my life noticed that I was always scratching my head. Mom had moved to San Jose already and maybe she would have noticed. She wasn't around so this is something we'll never know. Anyway, the troop was taken to Disneyland and with all the sitting next to the other scouts on rides, I managed to lice up all the girls' heads. Finally, after every girl was lice-free, I was forgiven. That is until we went to Knott's Berry Farm. After a nice day, we all went to the gift shop. My dad hadn't given me a lot of money to spend and there were two things I wanted. There wasn't enough money to buy both. So I purchased one item (I honestly can't remember what it was) and stole a journal by slipping it into my bag. I figured that hiding it in the store bag I had, it would look like it was something that had been bought. During the slipping the journal in my bag, I didn't notice one of troop members watching me. For some reason she didn't say anything right there and then. She tattled on me on the bus ride home. When I couldn't produce a receipt the journal was taken away. As the tattler's reward, she was given the journal and as my punishment I was asked to leave the Girl Scouts. That would be the first time I was banned from an organization. All this did was teach me to be stealthy enough to not get caught. To this day, I'm not sure if the leader told my father what I did to get kicked out. There are only two things I know for sure: 1) He never talked to me about the evils of stealing and 2) I was given a journal for my sixth grade graduation.

Let's back up a bit and start with my parent's divorce. My parents should never have gotten together in the first place. If they hadn't though, I wouldn't exist and I like existing. It's just they caused each other a lot of pain.

Shortly after my parents were married, Mom was told she'd never have kids by a doctor who obviously didn't know what he was talking about. My parents were high school sweethearts starting in their senior year and they waited until they were 20 to get married. Two years later, Mom became pregnant with my sister. It was a joyous occasion. Then three years after my sister was born, I came along. It seems that my parents' marriage started to go downhill after I was born. The fighting began. Mom would later tell me that by the end of the marriage, she didn't recognize herself in the mirror because her life had become about hurting Dad and not about enjoying life as she had wanted to. Three years after I was born, my brother came along. Mom had hoped my brother would help save their marriage but babies usually can't fix a relationship that is already broken.

Major tension ensued after my brother was born. Tension that as a young child, I picked up on. One day, when I was 5, my father and mother sat me down to tell me they were separating. My first thought was "good." Then they told me it wasn't my fault. I sat there silently thinking, "Oh, I know." What I said was "okay." My sister, brother, and I were sent to our babysitter's to live for the summer while Mom and Dad figured out their separate living arrangements. Dad found a place before Mom did and so we moved in with him.

A little while later, my mom found a job in the Bay Area and she packed her bags and moved from Bellflower, California to San Jose, California. A couple of years later, after graduating elementary school, I followed her. There I lived with Mom and step-father all by myself for about six months. Those six months as an only child started the best two years of my childhood.

Yes, I said step-father. One would think after the misery that was my parents' marriage, Mom would've been hesitant to marry again. She did find a gem of a man who loved her unconditionally until the day she died. They were married when I was 8 and on their wedding day, I asked him if we should call him "dad" and he responded, "You have a dad. I used to call my father Pop and you can call me that if you'd like." He's been our Pop ever since.

Bellflower during the 1980s was not the safest of places to live. The only solace I had growing up in that town was it was safer than the neighboring town, Compton. I didn't realize at the time, but the knowledge my hometown was safer than Compton wasn't something to brag about. Crime was everywhere. There was a drug problem among the student body at my elementary school. I was made fun of, because at the age of ten, I was still a virgin. Just a sad stinky place to live.

Elementary school was not the greatest place for a young bipolar child with a suffocatingly judgmental father at home. I often faked being sick to get out of class. I became very good at pretending to vomit. In the middle of the day, or sometimes at the beginning, whenever I felt my mind would explode, I would run to the restroom and come back to say I threw up and needed to go home. It happened so often, the teacher started sending a classmate after me to listen in on the visit to the restroom. I would put on a show worthy of any award. I kept up this act for the last three years of elementary school. The teachers I had during those years all failed me. Never once did they question why I vomited so much, or why I was faking vomiting, because let's face it, their suspicions about me faking it were spot on.

Dad's yelling and insistence I follow every one of his rules, even the easy ones, left a scar in my heart. This scar is from a wound that runs deep. Nothing I did or said mattered to anyone and I was constantly reminded of this. Thus, I became unfailingly polite. I don't want to intrude on someone else's existence. I don't want to be a bother. This politeness doesn't always work in my favor. I tend not to speak up when it comes to my own unhappiness. When I did speak up as a child and try to stand up for myself, Dad would yell at me. I took that action with me into adulthood and thus, rarely speak up for myself. Not saying "I'm sorry" for every little thing is still something I work on. I tread lightly in situations involving other people. I simply don't want to piss anyone off, so I'm nice to a fault.

Not all my childhood memories of my father are bad. One time he sent me to the store to buy a couple of packets of Kool-Aid and I came back with ten packets. He calmly sat me down and explained a couple means two. There were times he indulged my oddness. When Disney's The Little Mermaid came out, he bought me the McDonald's Happy Meal Ariel and filled a bowl with salt water, at my insistence, and let her live there. He never knew the Ariel toy told me out loud that that's where she wanted to live.

He always had food on the table. Normally it was fast food, or hot dogs, or mac and cheese, or some other form of junk food, but we always had something to eat. Mom couldn't even keep close to living up to that end of the parenting bargain. Sure, she was the better cook, but she totally mastered the art of the do-it-yourself dinner (which meant my siblings and I had to fend for ourselves for food) because she didn't want to prepare anything.

Not all of my childhood was horrible. In front of our duplex in Bellflower was a great big tree I loved to climb. This was back in the day when I had no fear of heights. My other friend in elementary school was a next-door neighbor and we had a lot of wonderful times up in the tree. In fact my friend and I had a lot of fun, period. She didn't seem to mind that she couldn't really believe a word I said. We enjoyed each other's company immensely. She also didn't seem to mind that I brought a stuffed dog with me for sleepovers. I never told her Krismutt talked to me- the limits of her friendship could be tested only so far.

In elementary school, I also developed my love of reading. It started with Nancy Drew. Nancy Drew taught me the magic of books. In sixth grade my school held a reading competition. I won the gold medal by reading fourteen books in fourteen days. Though I'll confess to you, most of the books I listed as reading in one day had already been read.

Yes, I lied in a reading competition. It's not something I'm proud of but the manic in me needed to win the competition and that mania convinced me cheating was the only way to win.

For as long as I can remember, Mom told me I was Irish. She decked me out in green every St. Patrick' Day. She said I was Irish through and through, well, except for the Italian in me. She even taught me how to make potage, a family Irish dish. My aunts later insisted they don't know where the potage recipe came from. A few years ago, I found the potage recipe alright, but in Julia Child's Mastering the Art of French Cooking. It's all a mystery why she'd pass a French recipe off as Irish, and didn't help me when I had my first grand delusion. I found out later that I'm not Irish.

I was in so little control of myself that I took every opportunity to be calm. Including illicit ones. Time consumers were shoved aside so I could calm my mind down. I was already great at faking being sick to get out of school. I also became a champion at not doing my homework.

In the elementary school I went to for every three straight days you went without doing homework, one detention was given. For every three straight detentions given, you would be suspended. I was suspended twice in 6th grade.

Detention was fun and suspension was even better.

With detention, I was to report to the cafeteria, and was given a chair to sit in. It was then expected of me to stare at a clock for half an hour. This was my chance to sit and calm my mind. Staring at a great big clock helped in the process. The poor educators didn't realize I wasn't doing my homework because I needed my mind to calm down or that my punishment actually gave me what I needed. Time to sit still and be calm. Suspension was supposed to be a worse sort of punishment. I was put in a cubicle in the library and given a few worksheets to complete. My only break was for lunch, that I also had to take in the library cubicle. The whole punishment scenario was a joke. I LOVED being suspended.

After my second one though, I was pulled into the principle's office and told if I was suspended again, I would be suspended for a week at home and it was made clear a week's suspension was serious and I was on the path of expulsion. I didn't want to face the shit storm that would happen at home if I was expelled so I began doing enough homework to never get detention again. In fact, throughout middle school and high school, I only received detention twice. I don't remember exactly what I did but I had become such a mild-mannered student that when the high school detention happened, the look of shock on the face of the teacher on detention duty was priceless.

My sixth grade year also brought one of my greatest memories. It was sixth grade camp. For one week, all the sixth graders were bussed up to a camp. It was freeing to escape the stress of my life and to just be alone. Well, alone with fellow students. It wasn't really hell to be trapped with my classmates on a mountain for five days. On our last night there, I cried because in no way did I miss home. In fact I dreaded it. It made me realize I needed to move in with Mom.

I wanted away from Dad but I also wanted away from Bellflower. The assigned Junior/Senior High had reported drive-by shootings, were riddled with drugs, and other activities that positively scared the crap out of me. Mom had left Bellflower behind and offered me an opportunity to have a peaceful school experience.

This still didn't stop me from having a full-on freakout about moving to San Jose. I ended up in the school's nurse's office having a panic attack because I didn't want to move away from my home. I'm a creature of habit and I don't like change. My mind is/was always changing between mania and depression. I needed to not have my outside world be unstable too. A new school in a safer city scared me. Even though I didn't want to experience the evils Bellflower had to offer, I was used to having drug warnings for my parents to read pinned to my shirt.

At the age of 11, I was tired. Tired and mentally exhausted, I knew moving in with Mom was the only good decision to make.

The little girl inside me who was used to that way of life is long gone. Gangs now terrify me. I refuse to go back to my hometown. It's enough that Bellflower lives in my memory. My childhood doesn't play a big part in my thoughts. It took me a long time to not dwell on the negativity of those years but neither do I look back on them with rose-colored glasses. I'm rarely nostalgic for my childhood. It means my memory has moved on even if some scars remain. I tend to obsess over tiny details and I'm grateful to no longer have my childhood be part of my everyday mind noise.

Chapter Four

Middle School Was Mainly Okay

After the freakout at the end of my elementary school life, I moved in with Mom and Pop. That move was one of the best decisions I ever made. No longer was I under the scrutiny of my judgmental father. I lived alone with my parents. My sister and brother remained in Bellflower. For the first and last time in my life, I got to experience what it was like to be an only child. It was Heaven. Especially for me, the middle child. Mom and Pop didn't yet have the attitude that I could take care of myself and thus be ignored. I was pampered accordingly.

Once in San Jose, Mom made it a quest to teach the ghetto accent out of me. She'd say it's liBRARAY not liBERRY. It's ASKed not AXed. So on and so forth. I'm forever thankful for the grammar and pronunciation lessons. Now my accent is a general Southern Californian accent and not one from the dangerous parts.

During my seventh and eighth grade years, my brain was mainly stable. My stress-free existence lessened my bipolar symptoms. It was a nice break and it's a lesson that took a long time to learn, but a reduction in stress means a reduction in symptoms. There were still some outbursts of symptoms but largely my illness left me alone. Just the way I like it. The concept of a mental illness hadn't entered my life yet, so I thought the spastic, depressed, and anxiety part of my life was something I had grown out of and I'd never have to deal with that mental state again.

In the middle of my seventh grade year, I met Terri. Terri and I became friends almost immediately. Throughout our teenage years, we created stories of fantasy. There was one where I fantasized Terri and I were stuck in a forest and had to survive until help came and rescued us. I lived that fantasy in my head for a couple of years.

In the second semester of seventh grade, Terri was the eighth grade teacher's aide in the reading lab class I was in. She was quiet and sat at the teacher's desk reading. We didn't talk to each other at all. That is, until the time we were both invited to teen night at the local Mormon church. Somehow we got to talking and became fast friends. There were arts and crafts set up at a table and one of the crafts was puffy paint for shirts. I took one long-sleeve shirt and painted, "boys have vaginas and girls have penises" on it. Whatever came over me to write that sentence on the shirt was hilarious. Okay, what came over me was my orgasmic mania. That symptom barely went on hiatus. The fear of becoming pregnant was the only reason I didn't go around having sex. Unfortunately, the Mormon church volunteers did not find it funny and we were asked to leave. That's how I got banned from the Church of Latter Day Saints. The Mormon church is the second organization I was banned from. I eventually became better at controlling myself and adjusting my behavior to my surroundings.

For a year and a half, we were the best of friends. Terri was my first kindred spirit. We were friends when she convinced me to jump off her roof. After making a few lands, I became too scared to continue with the fun. There I was up on top of the roof too frightened to get off the roof by either one of the two means. I could jump off the roof or go back the way I came. Terri gave me encouragement to jump after witnessing my panic about going down the side of the house. I jumped and landed on my left arm. Pain engulfed my body and I lay there assessing where the pain came from. Yes, yes, it's my left elbow and it was most likely broken. Terri came rushing over and I calmly told her to call my mother, gave her my mom's work number (this was the time before cell phones and everyone just had a rolodex in their head), and to get me an ice pack. Terri came back out of her house stating that she had called my mom and in her hands she had a bag of frozen peas proclaiming this was the closest thing she had to an ice pack. My mom came and helped me off the ground and into the car. The pain was so great it was easier to stay where I was. I contemplated lying in that position on Terri's lawn indefinitely.

An x-ray showed that I had broken my elbow into pieces. Surgery was scheduled and pins were put in. The cast my arm was in was itchy and basically my overall mood was terrible for six weeks. When the cast came off, the doctor took out the pins. That's a pain I remember to this day. The shock of the removal was massive as the doctor had lied to my face and told me it wouldn't hurt at all. That lie and the one about being able to eat ice cream after a tonsillectomy still annoy me when I think of them. That was the last time I went on a roof.

Terri and I would lay on the grass and watch the sky and let sunshine play on our shoulders (John Denver had sage advice). We watched a lot of PBS. Where in the World is Carmen San Diego and Ghostwriter were the two shows we always made time to watch. The only reason I'm halfway decent at geography is because of Carmen San Diego. Terri listened to The Beatles more than I cared to and I would repeatedly make her watched Ladybugs. Fun Fact: I can't stand the Beatles. I respect their place in music history and how influential they are but please don't make me listen to their music. Their music drives me to want to hurt someone. That sounds harsh and like an overreaction. Let's face it, I'm not good at having the appropriate response to situations.

A year after the roof incident, I woke up with a huge pain in my stomach on the right side. By this time Mom and I got to the ER the pain was on my left side. The ER doctor ran some tests including a pregnancy test. I was 13 and horrified the doctor even asked me if I was sexually active. I knew some kids in at my school were but well, I'm a goodie two shoes. Plus, my first recurring paranoia had set in. Now I had yet to do any baby-making action but it didn't stop me from believing I was pregnant. Soon enough, I realized when the fear would pop into my head and two days later my period would start. It was like clockwork. The tests results for my abdomen pain all came back negative and the ER doctor sent Mom and me along our way.

For a month the pain didn't cease and food made the pain worse. Potatoes were the only thing that eased the pain a bit. I went on a potato-only diet. In my middle school years, I only weighed ninety-five pounds and only eating potatoes made me lose fifteen pounds (I'm also only five feet tall, so I just looked very little). I was in and out of the hospital with test after test being done and all of them coming back negative. My family doctor finally said they would need to do an exploratory surgery.

What they found was I had three hernias and my appendix had fallen into one of them. It was surmised I was born with the hernias. The surgeon told Mom that he only knew of one other case of this happening. That's my life, if I do have something wrong then it's more likely than not something exceedingly rare. Being prepped for surgery made me nervous. The anesthesiologist with my elbow surgery had given me too much anesthesia and I was groggy for longer than normal. For the hernia surgery, the surgeon allowed my mom to be in the operating room (she was a radiographer who knew the surgeon). She gave a firm talking-to to the anesthesiologist about how much to give me. It eased my worry to have my mom with me as I was wheeled into the operating room.

The operation was done laparoscopically and since it was 1993, my abdominal muscle was cut. No one told me this but because of the muscle cut, if I ever had kids, I was going to need a Cesarean to give birth. Pop told me years after my oldest son, Theodore was born via emergency C-section, that because of the hernia surgery, I would always have to give birth by C-section. That was useful of Pop. Yes, I'm being sarcastic. (My mom passed four years before I became pregnant with my first child. Maybe she would have told me. Really, who knows?)

It took me a few weeks to be able to stand up straight and walk. My father even came up from Southern California to see me. Though he swore later he didn't even know about my surgery. I don't think I hallucinated his visit but I was hopped on some pretty good pain medication. He either forgot or my memory stinks. Who knows.

I had missed so much school that spring, I almost failed the semester. Mom talked sternly with the principal and somehow I managed walk in the middle school graduation with my fellow classmates without doing any make up homework. This wasn't a good lesson for a teenager.

Having said all this my middle school years were some of the best years of my life and that's because Terri was my best friend. For a year and a half after meeting, my life was mainly perfect. The Halloween during my eighth grade year, Terri and I decided to go as victims of a fatal car crash in the 1950s. We had a lot of fun making poodle skirts (To be honest, we conned Mom into making the skirts. We helped by keeping her company while she worked.) and Terri and I had a blast with the makeup. We were truly horrific looking and laughed the entire time we were out trick or treating. For all of you who think teenagers shouldn't trick or treat, I say to you: teenagers have some of the most creative costumes. Our 1950s car crash victims is a fine example of that.

During the summer before high school, Mom and Pop announced we were moving to Washington state. I didn't want to go. I might have even asked if I could move in with Terri. Well, no matter what I asked, we moved to Washington. That's when the letter writing began. Terri's letters made high school a little easier. Mom never had a problem buying me stamps for all my letter writing needs. Which I still appreciate to this day.

I'm not saying that there weren't any hiccups with my mental disorder in middle school. I was manic often enough, but it was easy to blame it all on the large quantity of Pixie Stixs I consumed.

If you don't know what Pixie Stixs are, let me enlighten you (I'm honestly not trying to be condescending. I don't know everything in the world, like do Pixie Stixs still exist? I also doubt I'm going to look in the candy aisle at the grocery store to find out. I'm that lazy. My point is, I'm not being condescending. I'm trying to be helpful if you're unaware of what Pixie Stixs are). They are sticks full of flavored sugar. It's seriously sugar that has been flavored. No lie. However, there were times when Pixie Stixs were not the culprit.

There was also the occasional loathing of myself. When I got my year book for my seventh grade year, I opened up to my picture and wrote "ugly bitch" over my face. Mom saw it and I lied and told her I had no idea who had written that. Mom became enraged and almost went down to the school to demand a new book, but I talked her out of it. I wasn't really disturbed by what I had done but I was at the fact that my mom didn't recognize her daughter's handwriting.

A decade and a half later, Dad made the same mistake. When I was in high school Mom went through a jam-making manic phase. I'm quite sure Mom was undiagnosed for bipolar. She knew she had depression but never caught on to her mania. Anyway, I was set to the task of labeling the jars with a sharpie. After she passed, Dad found a jar that Mom, for some reason had given him. He gave it to me as a kind gesture. He said he saw the jar and looked at the label and knew it was Mom's by her handwriting. I took the jar and looked at the lid. Crap. My father didn't know his daughter's own handwriting either. Mom's handwriting was way better than mine and it's not likely anyone could confuse the two. I'm a good child, I always send him birthday cards and Christmas cards, but there it is. Oh well.

I don't know what possessed me to write "ugly bitch" across my picture. It was a moment of despair. I had a great friend in Terri but I had once again become the middle child with a severe case of middle child syndrome. My sister and brother had just recently moved in with Mom, Pop, and me. What I kept hearing was "Meaghan can take care of herself." Take care of myself I did but, like most middle children will tell you, I didn't want the burden of being ignored. The six months I was an only child had come to end and I wanted it back. I wanted my parents' undivided attention.

I continued to have moments of fun just between Mom and me. On Mom's thirty-eighth birthday (when I was twelve), I bought a nine-inch round layered cake and put thirty-eight trick candles on it. If you haven't heard of trick candles, let me take a moment to explain. (I've been informed that most people know what trick candles are but do they really? A few years ago, I tried to buy trick candles and the candles were nowhere to be found. I got the feeling they were specific to late-twentieth-century novelty items, hence the explanation.) They are birthday candles that after being blown out, light themselves back on fire. I lit them all and walked into the kitchen where Mom was and said, "Happy birthday, Mom!" Her expression was of horror and ran to blow out all of the candles. She was successful and relief came across her face. That is until all the candles lit themselves back on fire. I started laughing really hard and Mom hurriedly took the cake from my hands, threw it in the sink, and turned on the faucet. The smoke detector went off and I fell on the floor at the hilarity of the situation. Mom turned off the smoke detector and looked at me. For a moment I thought I was going to be grounded until I was thirty, then she started laughing too and helped me up. She scraped off the burned frosting and we ate the cake.

At the beginning of my eighth grade year, the torment of being different from my peers started to gnaw at the fiber of my being. Terri was in high school. The other kids never teased me, or at least not to my face, but it was obvious I didn't fit in. This feeling of being an outsider clouded my school work. I was a B/C student but I was quickly becoming a D student. As my school work began to suffer, I started to beg Mom to get me a full time tutor so I could be homeschooled. I even wrote on the family calendar "Get Meaghan a tutor" on it everyday for two months. Mom just ignored my request. She never talked to me about my desire to be homeschooled. She shut me down when I tried to explain to her the misery of school. It's odd to me that she never wanted to know why I wanted to be away from my classmates. After a few months, I gave up and stopped asking.

That being said, middle school wasn't the worst time of my life. The memories probably seem like a string of (hopefully slightly humorous) vignettes that are relatively unconnected to my illness. I feel lucky in that way. It almost makes up for how stupid high school was. Note, I said almost.

Chapter Five

Looking for Space

I know how I'd commit suicide. Exactly how is not something I will ever tell because maybe someone will try to kill me and make it look like a suicide. Though, the lack of knowledge on the world's part leaves the assassin with a chance to be creative. I'll take that chance. I know how I'd commit suicide because I gave it a great deal of thought during my teen years. In my mind, you're not old until you're eighty-five. I don't ever want to be old, so my dream is to die at eighty-two on a rainy day. I plan on taking a nap I never wake up from.

Whenever life became too much, I would lie in my bed and imagine that I would die young. Sometimes it was by my hand but most of the time it would be from some traumatic illness. Then I'd imagine my funeral and the fantasy of the funeral would bring me comfort. To be free from my mental pain was very enticing. Never in my fantasies would anyone be overly distraught that I had passed away but I liked to think what nice things each person in my life who I cared about would say about me. This helped me through the paranoid belief that everyone hated me. If I could imagine everyone in my life had at least one nice thing to compliment me on, then I wasn't completely hated.

Teenagers tend to feel so intensely that everything is a life and death situation because everything is new. I was no different. Feelings that were never felt before became urgent and painful. Hopefully at some point a young adult realizes they will most likely grow old and as life repeats itself, they calm down.

I realized I was in for the long haul my junior year. The realization didn't make anything easier, especially with my illness. I didn't know how I'd survive until I was eighty-two with the way my mind worked. I still hadn't had bipolar disorder described to me yet. I just put my faith in a dream of a life not always being as crazy and challenging as my childhood.

It was my senior year in high school where I first heard the term bipolar. A therapist came to my current events class and talked about mental illnesses. He covered depression and ADHD. Then he began to describe bipolar and I thought, "Holy shit, that's what's wrong with me." I approached the therapist after his presentation and told him of my self-diagnoses. He gave me his card. I convinced Mom to let me see him. At the time, even though I wanted help, I wasn't sure how to help myself through therapy and spent my sessions talking about normal high school problems. Like how the boy I loved barely noticed me. The counselor pressed me to talk about what was going on in my mind. I wanted to so much, but I was afraid to. I didn't want to be judged based on the noise in my head. I was trying hard to appear normal, even if it meant not taking the help I needed from a professional who was there to listen.

Mom became tired of taking me to my sessions. She didn't approve of me seeking help. This is how God made me and why mess with His plan? This is a statement she repeated her whole life. Though, after she stopped taking me to see the counselor, she started seeing him herself. She told me this much later and I'm still confused as to why it was wrong of me to seek help but it was okay for her. She didn't do much to help understand her own illness. She said she saw him for six sessions and pronounced herself to be cured.

The only way to get to and from the appointments that were in the next town over from the small town we lived in was to take the bus. I have a deep unfounded fear of buses.

It didn't take long for me to cease therapy after Mom stopped taking me by car because of the whole bus thing. Okay, I don't like strangers. On top of that, my mind starts to play tricks on me that someone on the bus is going to follow me at my stop and murder me in a back alley. This paranoia deeply disturbs me and I avoid buses at all cost. Hence, I stopped going to therapy. It would take me many years to learn how to best utilize therapy. The bus fear aside, I simply wasn't ready to bare my soul to a trained professional.

One bit about me that made it possible for me to complete high school was this reserve of sheer will power I had. With each episode, my reserve would deplete a little. I knew one day the reserve would run out but I figured I could fly by until high school was over and deal with the drained reserve at a later date.

Here's a confusing transition. I'm about to talk about my freshman year in high school. My brain moves all over the place and to organize it in any other way then the way book is presented makes my brain hurt. Here's the start of my freshman year of high school: just as I was looking forward to starting high school with Terri, Mom and Pop moved us to Washington state.

The very first time I walked into the school, the size of the school caught my attention. The school was small enough for everyone to know each other. It made me uncomfortable. I like to be left alone and for the next four years that level of solitary I wanted was not to be. In San Jose, I would be lost in the enormous student body and I would blend into the scenery. That suited me just fine. High school is Hell for most people. I was one of the unfortunate few to have found my Hell on the first day as a freshman.

To be completely honest, the small-town high school I went to was the second one I was sent to. When we first moved to Washington, my parents put me in the high school nearest to my mom's work. We were living in a hotel (which wasn't sad at all) because we hadn't found a place to rent yet and Mom's job had started. Naturally, Mom assumed we would find a place to live near the school. She worked close to the school, in an even smaller town's hospital and she didn't want that big of a commute. The school was great and I started to make friends. Making friends was/is hard for me and the sheer fact that everyone was very welcoming, it made me feel very welcomed. I felt I belonged. Yes, yes, yes. It's odd to want to be a loner in one school and to have the opposite feeling at another school. It all depends on the company around me. Then my parents found a place for us to live a town over and I was dumped into a neighboring town's high school a month after school had started. Her commute was greater but after a few weeks she wanted out of the hotel and to have a place to call our own. Who knows, maybe the first high school would have ended up being terrible too but obviously that's a question I'll never have answered.

So, what happened my first day at the new high school that will forever be the event that started my frustrations as a teenager? Well, I was the new girl and no one really talked to me. Which is normal for every child transplanted in the middle of their childhood years. I missed my friends, my hangouts, and the mostly stress-free existence I had in middle school. On the first day at the new school, my brain wasn't causing chaos. I was having a very normal experience. I was all ignored and stuff. Ignored by everyone, except one girl who tried to hook me up with a boy I just met because she felt we would be perfect for each other. This level of need to match make and to be boy crazy left me cold. I wanted to be boy crazy so bad. I wanted to have sex to help with my orgasmic mania but I was also deeply fearful of becoming pregnant. None of this I shared with her so instead I was left with wanting nothing to do with these crazy people who felt the best life to live was a life with sex and drinking. The girl who set me up also told me she could get us beer. Alcohol is fun for most people and me (on occasion) but I don't like losing control and one of the main points of drinking is losing control. My desire to be left alone started to scream. I knew the possibility of me enjoying being at this high school was slim.

High school sucked, as I imagine it does for most everyone. Life at the small-town high school sucked. I keep using the word "sucked" but it never stops being accurate. I tried to make the best of it, but it was not the best place for me. I did make some friends and I fell in love twice (rejected both times) but high school is in the past and I rarely think about it. Except now. Only because I'm writing this book. Other than that, high school is no longer what defines me. I say to all the teenagers struggling to just make it through those four years- it gets better, or at least, moving on is a great thing and soon enough, it will all seem like a terrible dream that you never have to go through again. Just remember it well enough to have sympathy for your kids as they live through their teen years.

Here's a fun story that may illustrate my illness quite nicely. What it does is illustrates my motto of "never give up, never surrender!" (Okay, it wasn't my motto until I saw Galaxy Quest. It just fit so well, I decided to adopt it.) Shortly after moving to the small town, my sister borrowed my house key and promised to be home before I got home. Well, she wasn't and it was a cold bleak rainy day. Cold bleak rainy days are usual for the Pacific Northwest but for this newly transplanted Southern California girl, it was foreign weather. No one was home and there was no one scheduled to come home anytime soon. I tried all the points of entry and every one of them was locked. The garage, however, was open and I went inside to see if there was something I could use to help me get in. I saw the ax, and decided to go for it. I brought the ax to the back door and hacked off the doorknob. Ah, the warmth of the house was sweet and beautiful. Mom laughed and she made Pop see the humor in the situation. That weekend the door was fixed and an additional key was made for my sister.

One of the first things I did after getting my bearings was join the drama club. Drama wasn't high on the list of cool things you could do in this particular small town school. Some of my worst memories came out of my four-year tenure in the club. The kids in the club were outsiders and I quickly became the outsider of the outsiders. This realization came to me one night at a drama club gathering. For some unknown reason a couple of members busted out singing the song The Cat Came Back. I wanted to scream, because I can't stand the song. Instead I went outside walked in the giant backyard, and laid down in the grass and looked at the stars. I could hear the song still being sung and I cried. I wanted high school to be easy or at least not hell. I knew as I watched the stars that night and successfully did not punch anyone in the face that high school was going to be some of the worst years of my life. An overreaction? Possibly, but on top of usual teenage melodramatics, I was dealing with a disorder I didn't yet understand. I wanted to just fit in the way I did in San Jose and to some extent Bellflower. It wasn't really that I fit in, I was just accepted and I feared that night looking at the stars that being accepted wasn't something that would happen to me.

I can't act so I found my home doing tech. Which was fine. It's just the kids in the drama club were so elitist. I still don't understand why they had such sticks up their butts. I spent all four years of high school in the drama club and their treatment towards me should have made me quit. I wanted to be close to entertainment in whatever fashion I could be. I suppose it's time to mention my life goal of being a film director. That's all I wanted to be since seeing E.T. as a young child. I didn't want to act, I wanted to make movies. Being the one behind the camera had a great appeal to me. Many times in the drama club I was left wondering: What am I? Horse shit? Ah. I very rarely think of those people anymore. High school is behind me and that's something to be thankful for. I seem to be grateful my past is in the past. I simply don't have a lot of fond memories from my early years.

One shining light from the drama club was meeting Melanie. We met freshman year and have been friends ever since (we met in 1993 and it's now 2019). It's good to be at an age to have a few friends I've known for over twenty-five years. It's only going to get better. Then we'll all start dying on each other and that will be sad. Hopefully that is a long time from now. Death is something of which I am hyper-aware. No one knows when death will come for them. I'm a little morbid about it but I try not to be. It's life's great mystery and something that will never be answered. That is until I die but then I can't come back and explain death to anyone.

Back to Melanie, I wrote a song about her called 'Prozac' because that's how strong her light is. You can't be anything but happy when you're in her presence. We went everywhere together. In my senior year, I started staying over at her house on school nights because she lived one block away from the school. It solved the problem of me needing to take the school bus (yes, my phobia involves school buses too. School buses are in a prime position to kill many children all at once. That or the driver could be an undetected serial killer.) or my mom finding the time to drive me to school. Melanie and I would lay awake talking and laughing. It was perfect.

During our final year of high school, we took independent study together the hour before lunch. Soon into the school year, we started going to her house the minute independent study began and used perfectly good school time to eat English Muffins and play Super Mario World. One day, when heading to her house, the principal drove past us, looked at his watch, laughed, waved hello, and drove away. See, there are benefits to being a well-behaved student.

I wasn't a good student grade-wise. I was a solid B student, I just happened to be a well-behaved student. I might have gotten better grades if I tried a little more, but my main goal in high school was to graduate, not to be valedictorian. One subject that nearly derailed the dream of graduating was math. Numbers and my head don't mix. I had skated by in Algebra with a passing D+. The only reason I passed Geometry, the last math class I needed to take to graduate, was because the Geometry teacher, Mr. Ross, saw how hard I worked. I went to every study session he held. I should have outright failed the class, but Mr. Ross took pity on me and gave me a D. It helped that he was also in charge of the unofficial media club. I was the unofficial president as it was a class that was offered and not an actual club. However, I felt more at home with a video camera in my hand than talking through a headset backstage at a play. Mr. Ross knew I was a hard worker.

Melanie and I took French class together for two years. For two years we passed notes back and forth. To be honest, I didn't learn much French. I can say "Je suis une assiette de fromage" and more importantly "Je ne parle pas francais. Parlez vous anglais?" Which are, of course, "I am a plate of cheese," and "I don't speak French. Do you speak English?"

Back to the passing of notes. Almost at the end of the second year of French, Melanie giggled at something I wrote and our French teacher turned around looking furious. She snapped at us, "I know you two have been passing notes to each other for two years! It stops now!" I will never forget that. It was hilarious. Bad behavior is hilarious to me. Especially when I don't have to deal with it directly or, better yet, if I'm the one who's up to no good.

I don't remember my sophomore year in high school. The massive episode I had at twenty-two for some reason erased the year I was fifteen completely. I kept a journal faithfully and when I look through that year, my handwriting is there but none of the events register in my head as memories. To lose an entire year is unnerving but there it is.

There's actually another explanation as to why I don't remember my sophomore year. I used to joke there are twenty-eight personalities in me and they are all named Meaghan. Actually, there is really only one extra personality in me. Her name is Alternate Meaghan. I think she came to fruition in high school. She's basically a bipolar psychotic blackout.

What is a bipolar psychotic blackout? Let me tell you. It's a blackout that only bipolar people have. Got it? Good. Haha. I'll go into more detail. I'll start with explaining my blackouts. When I become really stressed out, I start to function on another level. I mainly spend money. It sounds stupid but in times of extreme stress, I will blackout and go shopping. I've lost up to two hours and have spent up to $150. Other people, will destroy their lives by cheating, lying, and spending money. All the actions they do, they don't have control over and don't even remember. It's frustrating and scary. It's difficult to know part of your life has been stolen by another person controlling your body. That's why I call her Alternate Meaghan. It's not me in control. The people who have witnessed Alternate Meaghan all swear she acts and talks just like me and they couldn't even tell it wasn't me. My blackouts usually don't involve more than spending money. At least I hope not. My manic episodes have never caused me to buy a car I can't afford. Nothing truly major happens with me, because as severe as my disorder is, it doesn't compare to the severity of others when it comes to this symptom.

Mom went by her middle name because she felt her middle name was more dignified than her first. She got it into her head that I should go by my middle name. I tried to honor her wishes. Thus when I started out at the second small town high school I introduced myself as Hilary. It took three weeks of everyone calling me Hilary to realize how much I love my first name. I'm like Anne Shirley in a way (Anne of Green Gables is one of my favorite books). She insisted on being called Anne with an E and I'm Meaghan with an extra A and an added H. When I say my name I see M-E-A-G-H-A-N in my head. I joke that my mom was feeling fancy the day I was born. Truth is no one knows how I ended up with the spelling. My birth certificate has the spelling Meagan. There has never been a good explanation as to why it was changed. Dad blames Mom and Mom blamed Dad as to how the mix up occurred. Then Mom changed her story and said it was meant to be Meagan and then her mom passed away. Since my grandmother was Irish, Mom wanted to honor her and gave me the traditional Irish spelling. When I told Dad this version he approved. It does sound lovely except it's a full of shit story. My grandmother wasn't Irish. In fact, no one is Irish in my family.

Tangent aside, I just wanted to be known as Meaghan and only Meaghan. I can't stand nicknames, for me anyway. If you call me Meg or Meggie, I'm probably going to ignore you. One other thing Mom changed about me was my last name. She registered me under Pop's last name. She wanted me to distance myself from Dad in as many ways as possible. For all Dad's flaws, his last name is mine and I wanted it to stay that way. Being thirteen, there wasn't much I could do about it. I changed my last name back after I turned eighteen.

Why we moved to Washington state in the first place remains a mystery. One day Mom pulled out a map of the United States and left where we moved to chance. She closed her eyes and pointed. Washington state was were her finger landed and then she started to look for jobs in the state and found one in western Washington. Where it rains during every season and there are only a few days of sun in summer. The sun in the small town was an even bigger rarity for me as I spent my summers with Dad. He lived on the Central Coast in California and spending summers with the beach within walking distance helped make up for the fact I had to live with my biological dad for three months. The funny thing about Dad was friends of Dad always said how proud of me he was. He has never once said to my face that he's proud of me. I like to think he assumes he's told me. Though, I may not have ever said I'm proud of him either. This pride thing may work both ways.

Before entering my senior year in high school, I entertained the idea of moving in with Dad. That's how awesome the call of the ocean was for me. I prayed for a sign of telling me what I should do and soon afterwards, I bought a doughnut, pink with sprinkles (the only doughnut I will eat. It's okay if the frosting is white, but the sprinkles need to be there), and in the frosting was a hole that was in the shape of the mascot at the small town high school. It was right there and then I knew I needed to go back home to Washington state.

During my senior year in high school, I took a zero-hour media class, which was a class that started an hour before school normally started. This is where I shone in high school. I was in charge of making the morning announcements via VHS. I took zero-hour media and an independent study media hour (The class Melanie and I skipped. We thought of a story for why we were going to her house without mentioning video games and English Muffins but no one ever asked and other than the principal catching us, no one knew). I still have some of my morning announcements up in my garage. These were my high school glory moments. I was awarded producer of the year and even made the local newspaper. That class was a ray of light in my high school years.

By taking the zero-hour class it meant my day ended an hour before everyone else's did. Mom worked the morning shift at the hospital and Pop worked the swing shift. Almost everyday after school, I met Mom and Pop at a local restaurant. There we would have lunch as Mom and I were done with work and school and Pop was heading to work. Every time I ordered a BLT with avocado and a blackberry Italian cream soda. That meal remains one of my all-time favorite meals. The hour we were at the restaurant for lunch, is one of my all-time favorite memories. We would talk and laugh and enjoy each others' company. It reminded me of the good times I had being an only child in middle school. After lunch, Mom would go home, Pop would go to work, and I'd either go back to school for an extra curricular activity or to the local library.

I volunteered at the local library. This was something I really enjoyed. The library was already my second home. The public library is where I discovered Lady Jane Grey and one of my favorite authors, Bradley Denton. I was looking up Cary Elwes and found a movie he was in before The Princess Bride called Lady Jane. I fell in love with Jane's story and was devastated to learn the movie isn't even remotely accurate. Once over the devastation, I read every bit of Jane's story I could get my hands on. I have read over five Jane Grey biographies and three historical fiction novels. Lady Jane Grey was the nine days queen of England back in 1553. She was fifteen years old at the time. When Queen Mary took the throne that was rightfully hers back in 1553, she threw Lady Jane in the Tower of London and Jane was eventually beheaded in 1554 after refusing to switch religions. Jane was only sixteen but she refused to convert to Catholicism like Mary had demanded. Jane stayed a true Protestant and thus was executed. It's a level of conviction I don't think I'll ever have about a religion.

I was doing research on Buddy Holly and found a book called Buddy Holly is Alive and Well on Ganymede written by one Bradley Denton. I checked the book out from the library and found I had stumbled upon one of the best writers few people know about. Bradley Denton's books are all fabulous and perfect. His book Buddy Holly is Alive and

Well on Ganymede remains one of my all time favorite novels.

Of course, the kleptomaniac in me and workplace politics ended my career. There was a spinner rack with paperbacks to check out. The books on the rack were't actually in the system and no one was really paying attention to how many came and went. It didn't take long for me to realize I could steal the books I wanted to keep. I told this to Melanie when we studying in the library. One of the employees overheard this. She told me every few months there was a book count. They have noticed the number of books have gone down. I knew she was being overly dramatic because at that point, I had only taken three books. Three books that I shouldn't have taken. I take full responsibility for my actions. I feared for my position for a few days. She didn't mention anything to the head librarian. I breathed a sigh of relief and vowed to never steal a book from the library again. She waited until she put in her notice and I applied for her job. I even interviewed for the job. I thought I had nailed the interview, plus I had been volunteering for six months and was actually doing a good job (aside from the stealing). About a week after I interviewed, the manager called me into the office. I thought I had gotten the job. Instead, the manager said a friend of the leaving employee was getting the job. Since I was stealing books, I was I was no longer welcome to volunteer. It went further than that. The manager banned me from stepping foot into the library. To this day, I still don't spend time at my local library. Shame fills my heart. Every time I step in a library, I'm reminded about one of my former worst qualities. It took a few more years but I did kick the kleptomaniac trait. At least to my knowledge, anyway.

I did fall in love twice in high school. The main love started at the beginning of my junior year, I was in my English class and the teacher called on a boy to stand up and answer a question. Michael stood up and I instantly fell in love. He apparently had lived in the small town his whole life but that was the first time I recalled seeing him. We slowly got to know each other over the next two years. Don't get your hopes up. The story ends in usual high school fashion. We never got together and didn't keep contact after graduation.

The voices in my head ramped up my junior year and there's one particular event that happened again and again and again. My belongings didn't want to be put on the floor next to my locker. If whatever I was holding was put on the ground it would start to scream a high pitched obnoxious scream. Whenever I had anyone near me, I would ask them to hold my stuff while my hands were busy with whatever task was occupying them. The person who was almost always at my side was Melanie. Melanie quickly grew tired of holding my items and soon enough I would say "Here hold this" and give her my stuff and she would put them down. Put them down I tell ya. PUT THEM DOWN! There was no freaking way I was going to tell her my stuff didn't want to be on the floor so I suffered with the screaming. For two years, my belongings screamed at me but seriously, I didn't want to admit to Melanie that I was a raving lunatic.

As much as I struggled during high school, I had graduating as a goal. Several times I considered dropping out. It was tempting to quit high school and focus on not going insane but I was determined to finish. Finish it I did. I have my high school diploma. I survived high school.

Chapter Six

The Day My Car Lit Itself on Fire

From my experience, being a young adult sucks. Being a young, poor, bipolar, retail working, lunatic adult really sucks. I had to work because college was not an option. My parents couldn't pay for college, so I didn't even bother applying. Mom sat me down my senior year in high school as I was looking at college brochures and told me not only that she and Pop didn't have enough money to send me to college, they were too broke to be burdened with a student loan to pay off if I couldn't find work right away. I couldn't imagine all that stress. Working and going to school at the same time felt like an impossibility. It's hard for me to do two things I can't stand at the same time. Even if I loved school, my attention would be diverted back to work. I have second to second mood swings.

Instead, I moved out of the house at eighteen and went to live with Terri in San Jose. San Jose might have been the moon with how much I was isolated from my family.

Okay, I didn't go straight from high school to San Jose. I started off my post-high school years living with Dad. I wanted to be in LA where all the Hollywood magic happened and I was willing to risk living with Dad (Dad often worked in LA and had a condo there). Dad told me I needed to get a job soon after moving in with him. The only job I felt I was qualified for was retail. This is all my fault. Dad tried to get me an office job but in my mind an office job felt like too much stress. I don't know what led me to this thought but there it is. I applied to a few stores in the Glendale Galleria. The only store that called me for an interview was The

Sharper Image (may they rest in peace) and they hired me. I was to be holiday help starting in late September with the possibility of being transferred over to full time after the Christmas season if I performed well. Let's just say, I did not do all that well and was told at the beginning of December that my my last day would be sometime in the first week of January. I told Dad this and he just nodded with no emotion at all.

After Christmas and before the New Year, I called Mom to say I was going to visit when I was let go. Dad had a habit of eavesdropping on my phone calls. Always. I couldn't have a normal conversation because I knew Dad would be listening in. To this day, I don't like it when someone else is in the room during a phone call. It drives me nuts because I still fear a lecture or a judgement because of what I said. Anyway, Dad overheard me tell Mom that I would visit and he yelled at me, telling me that I never told him I wasn't going to be transferred to full time. I didn't cry, I just stood there taking it and realizing something needed to change. I decided I needed to move out. Where to go then? The only friend I had was Terri in San Jose.

Terri and her mom gladly let me live with them. It was the only way I could afford to move away from home. Terri had already been entrusted with my secrets. She's the only person who has read my diaries because I allowed her to. It was exciting to bunk with her. We had perfect nights of giggling and talking and not sleeping. We were young enough to be able to stay up all night and not have the lack of sleep faze us.

Dad drove me to the train station and in another rare moment of honesty told me he knew he was a hypocrite and if I ever needed him, as long as it wasn't all the time and if the problem was reasonable, he would help me out. He also said that he knew it was my plan to move to San Jose all along and I just used him for room and board. This isn't the truth but after years of hearing this particular paranoia and denying it, I caved and lied to Dad by telling him he was right. Then he told me to go to church and sent me on my way.

Part of the difficulty of living with a mental disorder for me is not being able to work every shift. I have heard of the rare person with an illness who can handle perfect attendance. That's not in me. I'm a little lazy and am more than willing to take a mental day because I can't get past my laziness to suck it up and go to work.

It is a paranoia of mine that there's absolutely nothing wrong with me, it's just that I'm deeply lazy. However, as I write this I had to take an Ativan because I was hallucinating red bugs eating my brains.

There's nothing normal about that.

Throughout my work career I called in sick often. My mind couldn't handle the stress of working forty hours a week. The reality of always showing up was elusive. Days would pass where I couldn't get out of bed, get dressed for work, drive myself there and stand on my feet while handling customers. How was I suppose to not get fired? Somehow though, I have managed to never be let go in all fourteen years of bookstore service. I came close at different points but was able to cling on. The fact that I'm sort of proud of never being fired isn't really a thing to brag about.

Terri worked at Barnes and Noble and got me a job there. Having a friend recommend me for a job at their place of employment was one of my main ways of getting a job. Working at a bookstore is the best of the best when it comes to retail. Picking up books and dealing with snotty people seemed far better than working at any other type of store. This had already been proven as I worked for The Sharper Image, before moving to San Jose. It would be proven again when I took a second job at a comic book store. Still, book selling depleted my reserve of will power in three short years.

Upon starting a job, the first thrill for me was the first paycheck. When I struck out on my own there was no one telling me how to spend my money. I signed up for direct deposit and thought I was good to go. Best of all, I had been granted checks from my bank. This was back when writing a check to pay for your goods was not annoying for the cashier. Okay, it was annoying but so common that it came with the territory. I quickly discovered it took two business days for the check to clear. I was paid every Friday, so Wednesday was check writing day. I loved writing checks, it made me feel grown up. Shopping made me happy and it took me a while to figure out that my love for shopping was more like a chronic condition exacerbated by my manic episodes.

In a moment of confusion, while filling out my hiring paperwork for Barnes and Noble, I wrote that I was exempt from taxes. A few months after that, Terri looked at my pay stub and noticed no taxes were being taken from my paycheck. I didn't really understand what she was talking about and ignored her. Well, the next year rolled around and in doing my taxes, I ended up owing the IRS a couple thousand dollars. I told Dad about this because I was freaking out. I told him someone in accounting must've messed up and I did believe that at the time. I honestly didn't remember writing "exempt" until much later. Dad came through for me and paid my tax bill. I'll never forget how he helped me out in my time of need and I knew then that this was my one get out of jail free card from Dad.

The world should conform to me and not the other way around. I was fighting too much with the noise in my head to have to deal with things not being easy. I couldn't see or think clearly. People with bipolar have this problem. Well, this bipolar lady does anyway. Spending large amounts of money is a common trait and since the spending of money needed to happen as soon as possible, clear thinking eluded me. I imagine that clear thinking and problem solving tools are something only people with a normal brain have.

It didn't take long to realize the bank processed checks I had written before processing my paycheck. Checks bounced all over the place and I kept getting slapped with fees. I didn't think things through. If I had, I would have noticed the perfect solution to this problem. The solution was easy peasy pie. Write checks on Thursday. Spending money on Wednesday was stuck in my mind. I could not adjust my way of thinking to reality. My finances became a huge mess as the checks bounced. A few friends tried to explain the thing called bookkeeping. I was in no condition to listen. Numbers and my brain don't like each other and even if I had listened, I didn't have the concentration to sit down and do math. In the second Barnes and Noble I worked at, I was the cashwrap lead and was in charge of the store's money. I loved it because I could hide in the safe room and count money. I was responsible for the store's money and balanced out the totals for the sales five days a week. Somehow I could handle finances when it came to other people, I just couldn't manage the money they paid me for managing theirs.

After almost a year of bad check writing, the government (It was the government. I promise. I'm not making this up. I just don't remember what branch sent me the letter or even if was the state or the federal government) sent a letter explaining writing bad checks was a crime. Okay, maybe it wasn't the government who wrote the nasty letter I received but it was some sort of official group. No, I think it was the government. For some bizarre reason I didn't save the letter. That was a sarcastic sentence. I save letters but not ones with a negative association. This was my first warning and to clear my name, I had to attend a class that teaches how not to write bad checks. There were about a dozen people in the classroom, so I felt this issue was common and had nothing to do with the fact that my mental ability to function was slipping away. This class was one of the few classes from which I took away valuable information. I in no way wanted to go to jail. I was scared straight. The bad check writing ended. The whole Thursday thing became clear.

Terri and I finally saved up enough money to afford an apartment together. There we had the freedom of truly being on our own. Terri found a boyfriend soon after we moved into the apartment. On top of Terri wanting to spend all her time with her new boyfriend, I was always late with rent and in fact Terri had to cover for me several times. The whole concept of saving money was something that I couldn't wrap my mind around. I needed to spend money. I was high on mania and nothing compliments mania like spending money you think you're going to have. After around six months, Terri and I decided to go our separate ways living arrangement wise. She moved in with her boyfriend and I moved in with an asshat.

Another piece of history I try to forget is how much I stole in my early adult life years. I worked at a comic book store trying to pay off a loan I had taken to buy a car. I was so broke I couldn't afford to buy lunch, so it became a habit of mine to take $5 out of the till, fake a sale, and go buy myself a quesadilla. It didn't stop there. I stole items I wanted from both the comic book store and Barnes and Noble. I didn't do it for any thrills or because I could. It was all on impulse and it bothered me for two reasons: 1) because I was stealing and 2) because I would find items around the house that I couldn't recall buying or stealing. I wasn't ready to stare down the blackouts. The last thing I remember stealing is a book I really wanted from Barnes and Noble. It was a twenty-five-dollar book and I vowed I would never do it again. I could no longer reconcile my stealing with the type of human that I strive to be. I want to be a functioning member of society and stealing is not a way to go about being such a person. To my knowledge I haven't stolen anything since.

The owner of the comic book store knew what I was up to and for some reason never fired me. I deserved to be fired and/or have the police called on me. His silence while I worked there just led me to do it more. However, when I gave my notice via phone, he shouted, "Are you going to pay for all the stuff you stole!?!" and hung up. I never heard from him again.

Just because being a bookseller was a better job, for me than any other retail job, it doesn't mean it didn't come with its share of customers that were turd buckets. I have been called a bitch, a Jew hater, a racist, a stupid bitch, unfeeling, someone who will get cancer and diabetes and die because of my weight, and a waste of a human being. These comments I never really took personally but it would have been nice to not have to deal with those types of customers.

These were my wild years marked with more than retail stories and manic level of spending money. I met some dear friends with whom I was able to have wild crazy fun. No drugs were involved. Okay, underage drinking and illegally smoking pot (this was back when pot was illegal in California) happened from time to time. That's all. Barnes and Noble introduced me to the friends I had in those days. For that I will always be able to look at the bookstore and my wild years with great fondness.

The day Michaela came to work for Barnes and Noble, the manager announced her in the morning meeting by listing all the cool things she had done like travel to other countries. I felt as though I wouldn't even be able to talk to her because she was too good for me. There I was unable to cope with life in any meaningful way and she had accomplishments under her belt. Thankfully I was wrong. I could talk to her and Michaela was great fun. She didn't work at Barnes and Noble long and after her tenure, she became a manager at a cafe. I would sneak into her place of work after it closed and we would drink beer and use the oven to cook frozen pizza. Those nights are some of the best nights I have ever had. Plus, it felt grown up to be eating pizza and drinking beer. Michaela is a few years older than me, so she was only breaking the law by supplying me with the alcohol. We never got caught.

Michaela also introduced me to fancy restaurants. She would drag me to places where there was an actual dress code. Normally, the food was Italian. She would slip me the glass of wine she ordered. Ha! Michaela sounds like such a bad influence. She's my best friend.

Sharron started working at Barnes and Noble about six months after I did and we became instant friends. We had the same sense of humor and I enjoyed spending time with her. We would be crazy together. We'd drive around after getting off at midnight. For my birthday, I wanted to see Orgasmo, the new film directed by Trey Parker. We looked in the paper (this was way before you could buy the ticket and reserve your movie theater seat by purchasing it online) and saw that it was starting in about fifteen minutes, so we sped off to the theater and made it in time. This story doesn't seem all that exciting but it's time I mentioned my love of Trey Parker.

After watching Baseketball for the second time, I was smitten. In fact, I ended up seeing Baseketball six times in the theater, often with a friend and a scattered amount of other theater goers. Fun fact: I'm responsible for half of the final gross of the film. Sure, I watched South Park, but nothing compared to seeing Trey Parker on the big screen. He quickly became my favorite director and my fake boyfriend (the definition of a fake boyfriend is your main celebrity crush). I even managed to get ahold of a VHS copy of Cannibal the Musical. Even though my obsession with him is over, Cannibal the Musical remains my favorite movie. This is something I don't cop to all that often. Auntie Mame gets more respect when I say it's my favorite film. In all honesty, both movies are my favorite film. It's a tie and I can't choose between the two. I love them both a tremendous amount. One is a big-budget Hollywood movie and the other was made with sheer determination and both are amazing and hilarious. I love a good laugh and a movie that can crack me up after the twentieth viewing deserves the title of favorite movie. It's just that that particular type of hilarity is true for both films.

Back to Sharron. She accepted me when I told her about my illness. At the time, when I confessed my illness the response was normally "You don't have an illness" or, the even better one, "That's all in your head." She just responded with "That sucks," and she continued to spend time with me.

I was barely holding on to my sanity. My actions and words sometimes didn't make a lick of sense. One of my friends from middle school came into the bookstore wearing a shirt with a collar and a jacket with a collar. I started to lose control and focus and insisted one can't wear two collars and he needed to take his jacket off or put his shirt collar over his jacket collar. I know the story seems trivial but it's a good example of me losing the ability to think in a functional way. I became unnecessarily and oddly obsessed with his collars. To this day I can't tell you what I was thinking because I wasn't thinking. I was acting crazy but I wasn't able to tell at the time what a freak I was being.

A major pet peeve of mine is people sharing their music with those around them via their car stereo. After a shit day at work, John Denver was there to calm me down. I was not in the best frame of mind when at a stop light some jackass pulled up to the lane next to me blasting obnoxious music. My Toyota Celica Supra had a decent stereo system, so I turned up the volume to Rocky Mountain High. Yes, I got into a sound off war with a stranger. Obnoxious music vs John Denver. (I recognize for some people, John Denver is obnoxious) I finally turned up Rocky Mountain High to the highest level and then the light turned green. I sped away because, well I owned a sports car and my rival didn't. I need life to be easy and conflict free and without jackasses invading my head space.

Shortly after the John Denver showdown, I got into a car accident that would ruin the Celica and my life for a little bit. I was having a bad day and bad days usually don't mix with driving. I turned right into a parking lot and ran right into a SUV. It didn't help that I was crying while driving. My tiny sports car went right under the bumper of the giant SUV. The owner of the SUV wasn't mad for some reason and felt the need to say, "God works in mysterious ways." Which, I have to tell you, is not something that should ever be said to a crying nineteen-year-old right after she ruins her car. The Toyota Celica Supra was unharmed when it came to the engine but the left side frame was bent in such a way the wheel could't turn. The kind-hearted driver had a cell phone and let me call my roommate. When he showed up, he claimed that this wasn't great because I owed him a bunch of money. Then he left and a tow truck came to take my bent car home.

Then the nightmare began. The Celica was dropped across the street from the house. Fine, right? Nope. Across the street was an elementary school and where the Celica was, it blocked the parents from dropping and picking their kids up with ease. They quickly complained. Somehow the Celica was moved in front of the house. The neighbors complained about the eye sore of a wrecked car. Two things would have solved the problem to fix my car. One, the auto insurance could have helped out but Mom had let my insurance lapse without telling me. That was a fun conversation with the insurance company. They promised to pay for the damage of the SUV if I sent them money to make up for the lapsed insurance. However, under no circumstance would they pay for repairing the Celica. I only needed $500 to fix the frame. That was a lot of money for a broke person. Two, for some unknown reason that even he wouldn't explain my roommate could have let me park the car in the driveway until I could pay for the repair but didn't. I still can't think about him decades later with any fond memories.

There I was with no hope. Enough neighbors complained to the city, and after a few weeks of complaints, the city towed my car. My credit was too bad to take out a loan. I took out a loan to buy the car and I was making payments just fine. Then I went on a two month road trip with Dad (which probably makes me sound spoiled but there's a story behind why Dad insisted on me taking a hiatus and hitting the road with him. It's just I honestly can't remember what it was. I barely remember the trip.) and instructed my roommate to mail the checks at the allotted times. Why I was too stupid to not mail them myself has haunted me ever since. I have no one else to blame for my credit taking a beating but me. When I came back home, I learned my roommate had not mailed the checks and the bank sent me a notice to pay the whole loan back immediately. I negotiated with the bank and they agreed to let me pay off the loan in three separate payments over three-months' time. I begged and borrowed the money to pay off the loan. I took a second job to pay everyone back. The bank was paid back but my credit was shot. Thus, no loan to fix the Celica. Thus the Celica was towed.

All this time, I had to find friends to drive me to and from work. Somehow, I managed to not miss any days of work. Well, I called out a couple of times, so I managed to make it to all the shifts I was well enough to show up to. Then Terri's mother came to my rescue. I'm not sure if she knows how forever grateful I am to her but the gratitude will always be there. She had a beater she was going to donate. It was a beige 1982 Toyota Corolla Tercel. (I'm not joking. A lot of people have the need to explain to me the car was either a Corolla or a Tercel but I promise the car was a Corolla Tercel.) Terri's mother gave me the car for free. I had a car. That was a life-saving donation. A few weeks later the

Carola Tercel told me her name was Peggy Sue. Peggy Sue quickly became a good friend. She talked to me. She kept me company on the road when I was alone. She was fun and lively. I actually miss her jokes and voice. When it came time to finally donate her to a charity because she could no longer pass a smog check or drive past 50 miles an hour, I cried. A dear friend left my life that day.

As my well of will power was depleting, I got further and further away from controlling me. I became three layers. I became surrounded by fog (fog was my nickname for my disorder). There was me, Meaghan, in the center controlling my words and body movement. Sounds basic but a thick layer of fog was setting into the space between who I am (was? I can't tell. Tenses are tricky for me.) and how I moved and what words I said. The fog kept getting thicker and thicker. The ability to concentrate was fleeting. The person I am on the inside was getting lost and the fog was taking over. I could barely see more than a foot in front of me. Everything else was noise I couldn't handle. I literally kept my head down to avoid the fact that I wasn't able to concentrate on anything more than to stand upright and walk. Soon enough I was barely hanging on. Never once was control completely lost. Somehow a thread of sanity was keeping me from going over the edge. I became afraid but there was nothing I thought I could do about it. There wasn't a solution. I was hurling on to a path of destruction.

My mind was melting, focusing on a basic level of human function became a dream. What was my next move? How could I get out of this mess? What would become of me? Would my illness win and I'd end up in a mental facility for the remainder of my life? Let's face it, if I continued on the path I was on, it would win.

These and other thoughts filled my head as one day I drove down the road to get home. Then I noticed other drivers on my left side trying to get my attention. They were waving frantically and that's when I smelled smoke. I quickly pulled over into a parking lot and I got out to inspect my car. Sure enough, Peggy Sue's back tire was on fire. It felt like the universe was trying to get my attention. My life, along with my car, was on fire.

I have no memory of how the fire was put out or how I got home. I assume someone nearby had a fire extinguisher. They must have called a tow truck for me. It turned out I had neglected my car. Peggy Sue's break pads were gone on the back left passenger side. My roommate was irritated because I was a "stupid, naive girl." Then he replaced my brakes and added the labor (roughly two hundred dollars) to a tab he had been keeping.

It was an interesting day when I discovered this tab on his computer. The tab was over a thousand dollars. He never once told me he was doing this or that I needed to pay him what he felt he was owed. I have a bad habit of taking advantage of people, it's not something I'm proud of but still, he should have told me he expected to be paid for more than rent. The discovery helped me make up my mind to move back home to LA. The running tab consisted of everything from helping me move in to his house to having me pay for my birthday present. He never did collect his money. I should be ashamed of myself that I refused to pay him back but by the end of my San Jose years, I really couldn't stand him. There aren't any lovely memories in my head surrounding him but there is also a huge amount of guilt surrounding my behavior towards him. It was then and there that I decided to go home to Southern California.

One of the many issues with working was the massive amount of times I called out sick. I have only been written up once for all my absences. I remember this well because it was another reason I decided to move back to Southern California. If you wear glasses, then take them off (if you have no issues with your eyes, humor me and pretend) and experience the blurriness. Notice how you can't see what's in front of you all that well. I wore my glasses everyday but I was having a hard time making out shapes, objects, and faces. My eyes are corrected with glasses but my brain was out of focus. I wanted to cry as I sat there in the manager's office being written up. My head was spinning. My manager told me if I called in sick one more time, he would write me up. He must have changed his mind, because when I walked into work the next day, there he was waiting to write me up. I knew on paper it looked like it was time to fire me but paper doesn't always show the whole story. I was drowning and I couldn't figure out how to save myself. I was all alone and without the means to explain my situation. Our society, here in America, stigmatizes the mentally ill. Instead of lending a helping hand, it's easier to tear mentally ill people down. It's not productive and it isolates us even more by keeping us in the shadows. Taking a mental health day can look like I'm relaxing and being lazy but really, I'm just trying to give my brain a rest so I can live another day.

It didn't take long for me to pack up my things and leave my wild years behind. There was sadness saying "good-bye" to my friends, especially Michaela. No matter how far apart we were, I knew we would always be in each other lives.

There is a war between Northern California and Southern California. Northern Californians hate Southern California without anyone in Southern California knowing this or caring. I was relentlessly teased because I'm from LA. Apparently the way we give directions is wrong. We Angelenos put "the" before each freeway. Everywhere else in this country, if you have to give directions you say "take 5 to 210." However, us residents of Southern California say "take the 5 to the 210." I was mocked relentlessly in San Jose for this stupid nuance. All I have to say is if you can say "I'm going to McDonald's" or "I'm going to the McDonald's," does it matter if I am stating I'm going to take a freeway or the freeway to get where I need to go? There's also the matter of the history of the fabulous Southern Californian freeway system. I should explain Southern California had the nation's first fully integrated freeway system and they all had majestic names like "The Pasadena Freeway", "The Imperial Highway", and "The Pacific Coast Highway." Later it became the 110, the 90, and the 1. We Angelenos are trailblazers and our usage of "the" before freeway numbers is part of our culture.

Anyway, when I told people I was heading home, they would look at me with disgust and ask "why?" My answer was hilarious, at least, to me. I said, "To marry Trey Parker."

Chapter Seven

My Life-Altering Episode

Obviously, I didn't marry Trey Parker. I instead transferred to the Barnes and Noble in Pasadena. Melanie followed me as my new roommate and I got her a job as a bookseller. Melanie didn't have a car so we shared Peggy Sue. Melanie and I had many nights of laughter. One of us started writing love notes on the other one's lunch. I honestly couldn't say who started the love note writings but soon it involved into two fictional lovers named Bruce and Gary. We would try to one up each other in making the other blush.

About a week after transferring to Pasadena, I met Jonathan. A few months later Jonathan and I started dating. I realized I was putting a boy before a friend, which is what Terri did to me, so I knew how much of what I was doing to Melanie was lame. I was in love. A few months after Jonathan and I started dating, Melanie moved back home. Shortly after Melanie moved out Jonathan and I moved in together. This is literally how my mind remembers this period in my life. Six months in the matter of six sentences. I do imagine this is true for most people at some point in their life. Months can be condensed to a matter of sentences.

Somehow, I managed to be promoted to Music Manager at my fourth Barnes and Noble. I might've been good at my job but I was on a rollercoaster ride that I couldn't get off of. The stress of actually having to show up on a consistent basis because I had to manage an entire department depleted my willpower. That may have been okayish but the store manager was a great big meany who went out of her way to make my life Hell. I barely remember her. I just have an image of a gigantic turd bucket as I'm thinking of her now.

The best way to describe exactly what happened is to say my brain broke. I ran out of sheer willpower and my brain, like a beat up computer, broke down. Our brains are our own personal computers. It was like mine had been repeatedly hit with a baseball bat. I wanted to lie down and die. There were days when I almost did. For months I was in a near catatonic state. I was barely functioning. It would take eighteen months to get back to my brand of normal.

In December of 2001, I was working a usual Christmas shift, when I looked at the second floor of the two-story store and while I was ringing up customers at the register the book cases started to move. (Ha! How's that for a long sentence?) This was the first visual hallucination I'd ever had. None of the inanimate objects that talked to me ever moved their mouths. They stayed stationary. It's as though their voices came from a speaker and not by lips moving. That's one of the reasons it took so long for me to figure out not everyone had inanimate objects talking to them. It would also be the only visual hallucination I was to have for more than a decade.

I naturally freaked out and went to the ER. I didn't know what else to do. I was living by the seat of my pants and didn't have a psychiatrist. The ER doctor didn't believe me at all and sent me home. He wrote me a note for one day off work. My mental state became worse and I went on medical leave a few weeks later. I saw my general practitioner at the time and he recommended a psychiatrist who ended up being a nightmare. The psychiatrist was more about helping me by overmedicating me than listening to my hesitation in taking medication. I wanted help but his approach felt like an overreaction. We didn't gel well as a mental health team. I was scared and didn't know how I would react to the drugs he prescribed. This was my first time being serious about seeking treatment and I wanted to get it right. He admitted me to a mental hospital on my request. I was naive enough to have romanticized mental institutions. The belief that a hospital would be a relaxing and calm place to heal ran through my fantasies. My mind needed sanctuary and thus the idea of a place where my mind could find peace was concocted. I wanted a safe place to start taking medication. The doctor didn't warn me how awful mental hospitals are.

I had to share a room with four other patients and I have a deep-seated fear of sleeping near other people. I don't want anyone to see me sleep. I'm the most vulnerable when I sleep. At any moment someone could attack me and I wouldn't see it coming. Jonathan and I had been living together for about a year at the time and I still wasn't comfortable with the possibility of having him watch me while I snoozed away.

That was my first lesson in hospitals not being all I imagined them to be.

Everyday, us patients had to take at least two classes. One had to be a group session class. I'm nervous talking to other people and even more nervous talking about my illness. For my whole life I had cultivated a program of smoke and mirrors to deflect anyone being able to see how sick I am. There I was, placed in a circle, being told to tell my story. I was more than willing to listen to everyone's story but I in no way wanted to talk about mine. I'm also good at denial and part of me was in denial I was even sick. I asked for help but then help scared me. As a deflective measure, I started to roll my eyes at other people pouring out their story. This is more about me and my issues than anyone and theirs. Group therapy isn't for me.

The second class I opted to take was a musical circle. I was so strung out on the medications I was given, that I don't even know what instrument I choose to play. In fact, I didn't even know what medications I was taking. The psychiatrist never informed me of his treatment plan. I opted to go into the hospital but I lost complete control of my care.

I brought Krismutt with me as a comfort. I'm glad the nurses let me have him because they confiscated my toothbrush and mouthwash. The mouthwash was in a glass bottle and contained alcohol and I forgot you can make a weapon out of a toothbrush. Of course the medication silenced Krismutt but I pretended I could talk to him. I needed his conversation to help calm my fears of being in a room full of other people who were most likely sleeping themselves and not watching me. Now, sometimes I respond to the auditory hallucinations by speaking out loud and looking like a raving lunatic. I normally do this when I'm alone, because I don't want to look like a raving lunatic. Most other times, I speak telepathically. It worked and that saved me from acting like a person having a conversation all on her own. I talked to Krismutt everyday and he gave me comfort as I cuddled with him. Even though he was silent, I imagined what he would say. That's how well I knew him. I knew what he would say.

After six days, Jonathan came to visit me and I cried and begged for him to get me out of there. Yes, my stay had only been six days, but it felt like months. For some reason they wouldn't let me check myself out. I thought since I voluntarily checked myself in, I could leave at anytime. After some brouhaha because Jonathan wasn't a family member, they allowed me to be signed into his care. They made him sign paperwork stating that I was his responsibility and the hospital couldn't be held liable if I harmed myself or others.

Hurting myself or others is something that is not in me. That's a frustrating part of having a mental illness. It's automatically assumed that having a mental illness means you're violent. It doesn't. Most people living with a disorder are harmless. Sure, not every mentally ill person responds well to treatment or even seeks it. Their lives may not be the best lived but it's their one chance at life. We are human beings with a crappy condition that few people bother to understand.

Shortly after leaving the hospital, I found a therapist. She recommended a psychiatrist and he's been my doctor ever since. The day he retires will be a very sad day indeed. Then my doctor will probably be someone much younger than me and it will do nothing but remind me I'm no longer young. I want to grow old without actually having to grow old. I'm already starting to become a crabby middle aged woman with a disdain for the younger generation. I don't even have a generation. I'm not Gen X and I'm not a Millennial. I was doing just fine as Gen Y, so I'm sticking with that. Okay, that was a tangent. Not a big one, but one none-the-less. With a therapist and a doctor, who doesn't believe in overmedicating, I began the healing process. The healing process began six months after my hallucination of the bookcases.

I spent my days lying in bed with hardly enough energy to watch TV. One can fix a computer or in a worst case scenario buy a new one. As much as it would've been nice, I couldn't buy myself a new brain. The only course of action was to give my brain time to rest. Michaela came to visit me from San Jose a lot. I will never forget how great that was. She's the only one who seemed to care. My family abandoned me. Honestly. Dad tried a little but ultimately decided I was faking it. He bought a Christian video on bipolar disorder and watched it with me. The video explained extreme bipolar disorder and tried to teach friends and family to understand the bipolar sufferer just needed love and Jesus. It actually was a nice video that never once judged someone who has the mental illness. Since my illness isn't as extreme as the examples in the video he stopped attempting to believe me. Mom figured Jonathan was fine taking care of me. She didn't once come visit me. I couldn't take care of myself but the mentality that I could stuck with my family. She also tried to discourage me from seeking help. Since she didn't lay eyes on me for twelve months and that was when I went to visit her, she never fully understood how sick I was.

Everything is kind of a blur. The days melted into each other. I had the occasional good day. When that happened, I did nothing of importance, because a good day was so rare and I wanted to enjoy the peace in my head and not over stress my brain. Yes, on bad days I did nothing either so on paper it looks the same but was was going on in my brain was light years apart.

Laying on the couch or bed, a realization happened. I had lost memories. A lot of my childhood seems to be gone. It also felt like my brain had stopped creating memories. Not completely but a lot of fuzzy images filled my brain. I couldn't recall what I had done the day before. What I had eaten, what I wore, even what I did. As a teenager I played memory games naming what I wore and ate the days previous. I could reach back up to two weeks. The memory game became impossible to play. As my brain healed, my ability to remember became better. Even now though, that time in my life feels like it lasted only a month. Not the year and a half that it was. Not the year and a half that was stolen.

Yes, stolen. My brain, my illness, robbed me of a year and a half of my life. Poof, gone. With the passage of the years, this fact no longer bothers me. Okay, a little, but I accept it now. It's something that happened to me but I was able to move on.

Dad did come visit often to stay the night in our guest room when he needed to work in LA. Every freaking time he visited, he took me on walks around the neighborhood to tell me how much I was messing up my life. One common thread was how much I needed to lose weight. Oh, and I needed to get off my medication because I wasn't really bipolar. In fact no one is bipolar. The disorder is in my head and it's really mind over matter. Then he would pick on whatever else he could. These walks caused such dread in my life that I ended up refusing to let him stay the night as often as he wanted to.

In addition to the walks, I would hide whatever I could from him that might induce anger in him. I love the movie People vs Larry Flint. There was the time I forgot to hide it and Dad went through all of my films one by one, commenting on them before as he made his way to the P's. Then he yelled at me for owning a movie about a pornographer. I stood up for myself as best I could but there I was twenty-two and scared of my father. If Dad reads this, he'll be shocked and mad that I love Trey Parker. Strangers With Candy is one of my favorite shows and he'll only know that if he reads these words. His judgmental behavior led to him not really knowing his daughter. It's sad but it's a fact. I really wish I could be me but instead I painted a picture of a perfect women whose only flaw is not going to church. Which, let's face it, is a big problem with a Christian minister.

Getting back into the work field proved challenging. I found a job at Suncoast Video (may the company rest in peace). I thought it was perfect. I loved movies and all they sold was movies. It was anything but the place of movie greatness I thought it would be. I thought I'd get to sell movies but instead I was expected to up sell like crazy. Talking customers into buying more movies was never an issue. Having to also sell magazine subscriptions was torture. I can sell products when I believe in them. However, I don't like being forced to harass people and to waste their time by talking about a product that sucks. That may not have been such a huge deal, but my brain still wasn't functioning well and it became too stressful. Two or three weeks in, I quit for my own sanity. I felt my health slipping backwards. I was just coming out of episode that altered my life and I didn't want to retreat. The manager was furious. Apparently he wanted to promote me. That may have been the only time in my working history someone wanted to give me more responsibility in such a short span of time.

As my brain started to clear up, I convinced myself that Jonathan had asked me to marry him. It wasn't a grand delusion, like the ones I would have later in life, but somehow I started to believe a desire I had was real. I wanted to marry Jonathan and thus us getting married had to be true. It was very manic of me. It did cause me to apologize to everyone I put on notice about the upcoming wedding. Michaela came to visit and congratulated Jonathan and me, in front of Jonathan, for our engagement. Jonathan, of course, was startled and asked what she was talking about. Michaela excused herself to the restaurant's restroom. Jonathan asked me what she was talking about and I had to step out of my fantasy world and tell him I had been telling everyone we were engaged. I was nervous telling the truth. Truth is not my middle name. Truth is what I ended up telling and it pained me greatly. I can't remember Jonathan's reaction but since we actually did go on to get married, it couldn't have been too awful.

What exactly caused my life altering episode that would take eighteen months away from me? Nothing specific. It was bound to happen. I knew it was coming and even though I feared for my health there was nothing to be done. The massive episode was going to happen sooner or later. I was on a train barreling towards a cliff and I could either jump off (kill myself) or brace for the fall. I braced for the fall. The fall was one of the hardest things I've ever gone through. The fall was brutal and it took me a while to land and an even longer time to pick myself up. It may have lasted eighteen months but it took me a decade to stop fearing every episode would be the beginning of another life altering episode. I never want to go through that again.

Chapter Eight

Where Do I Go From Here?

One of the side effects of mental disorder medication is it increases your appetite, thus causing the taker to gain weight. Unless you go on an incredibly strict diet and do an insane amount of exercising to combat the weight gain. Which is not something I have the discipline to do. Being extremely overweight was a whole new experience for me. Sure, Mom had been a large lady and I loved her just as she was, but it's one thing to love a plus size person and be thin and to actually be a plus size person yourself. Over the course of four years, I went from being cute and thin to a loser who's fat. I never felt like a loser who's fat but that was something that was said to my face on more than one occasion. People would stare at me as I ate and being a paranoid mentally ill person, strangers staring at me was not exactly helpful. Later after graduating from college, I worked at the Barnes and Noble in Thousand Oaks, California and that's where the helpful people would feel it was their life's mission to let me know that because of my weight I was going to get diabetes and/or cancer and die. Fun for me. The worst part was as I gained weight, people I knew would pat my expanding belly and ask what was going on. When the weight started piling on, a few strangers asked when my due date was. It's demoralizing to have both scenarios happen as I struggled with the fact that I was gaining a massive amount of weight.

Mom was overweight and so I should have anticipated this increase-your-appetite side effect plus unfortunate genes would add on the pounds. My psychiatrist would tell me that a new medication would make me gain five to ten pounds and I would gain twenty. I went from a fashionable 120 pounds to 215 pounds in the matter four years. I'm only five feet tall and the weight didn't evenly distribute itself. I had to live by the theory that I'd rather be sane and overweight than skinny and in a mental hospital. Still it was very demoralizing to have the extra weight.

Now onto my college degree. What?!? I have a college degree! With my disorder and everything? Hold on to your excitement. I have a useless city college film degree. Haha. A lot of people with mental illnesses have graduate degrees and beyond. Homework and my brain don't mix very well. That and it's a requirement of most professors that students actually show up to class. I'm better at taking mental health days than powering through. With the episodes still coming and going and different medications being tried with interesting side effects, being a full time student who was actually a grade-wise good student was not in the cards for me. However, my degree is a source of pride. It took me six years to get my two year degree from Pasadena City College (PCC), but I do have it. After a year and a half of recovery from my life-altering episode, I felt stable enough to go to college. At first I was able to handle a full load of courses and work part time. I was living how I always wanted to live. Like a normal person with a normal brain with normal stressors. This lasted one semester. Then it all went down the toilet.

Vroman's Bookstore is located next to PCC and I got a job there. It had a major perk in that the clientele is wonderful and nice. However, it's the single worst job I've ever had. The second worst job I every had was at the comic book shop that I took to pay off the bank loan when I lived in San Jose. The comic book store was next to an adult movie theater. Back when I was nineteen and a tiny little wisp of a girl.

I shall take a moment to talk about the Vroman's clientele. I don't have obnoxious customer stories. Instead I have good stories. Like the man who wanted to buy his daughter good books but only in hardcover. It was a dream come true because he ended up buying fifteen hardcovers all of which were my recommendations. Okay, I'll let you in on a fact. Vroman's is in a rich part of town. The area is full of people with a lot money who are insanely nice and polite. Well, in my experience anyway.

One semester down and then I had another episode, and another, and another. I had to take my course load down from full time to part time. I had to quit working and still the episodes kept coming. I took an entire semester off the Fall of 2005 because of one giant episode. My episodes were bad but what made them worse was my fear of having another massive episode. I was overly cautious about my mental health. The most common episode for me is a mixed episode. I wanted to get out of bed, I really did but I couldn't because I was too depressed to be how manic my brain was begging to be.

In the Spring semester of 2006 I took a film making course in which I needed to make a 7-10 minute short film. I thought it would be hilarious to make a film about my high school love for Michael. I called it Hilary and Michael. It was hilarious and I was able to pull it together long enough for me to actually pull it off. Then I mentally collapsed again. Not to the extent as before but terrible enough for me to hide in my house and not come out for three months. In fact, I ended up withdrawing from school the following semester just to recover from the stress of making a short film. I tried to show up for classes in the new semester but I just couldn't get out of bed. I couldn't be there in any sort of fashion. The need to take care of my mind came first.

My two favorite customers at Vroman's were my Nancy Drew ladies. They loved Nancy Drew as much as me. Just for longer, as they were in their 50s. Whenever I found anything cool that had to do with the famous teen detective, they were called. I never got to introduce them to each other but a good conversation was had when one of them came in and we chatted about the definition of titian hair (It's strawberry blonde! No! It's simply plain red! I was on team strawberry blonde.) and I always found myself defending the Nancy Drew Files. That was the series from the 1980s and it got me into Nancy Drew in the first place. Though *gasp* the series included murder. Something Nancy had never dealt with before.

I learned a lot too. I hadn't realized that (surprise!) the versions of the first series that are in print today aren't the versions that were originally published. In the 1960's the originals were rewritten to make up for the times changing. I love to play the Nancy Drew computer games but only one of my Nancy Drew ladies did. The other acknowledged they help promote Nancy but she didn't like the idea of Nancy being reduced to a video game. (Nonsense! The games are fun!) Along with my two ladies, I was able to talk about Nancy with all ages. The closest I got to that at Barnes and Noble was a mother refusing to buy Nancy Drew for her daughter because the books were written in "Old English." She was referring to the books published in the 1960s not the originals published in the 1930s, which isn't even close to being in Old English. I couldn't stop a look of horror from spreading across my face. See, the customers at Vroman's were much better. At least, to this geek anyway.

After leaving the children's department on a permanent basis, I worked for three holiday seasons in the Will Call section of Vroman's. It was my job to retrieve customer orders and to gift wrap books. I'm not one to let customer insults get to me. I will now tell you about the one time someone did get to me. A woman dropped off her three gifts to be gift wrapped and said she'd be back in two hours to get them. I asked her where she'd like me to put the labels (every piece of inventory at Vroman's had a label with its

SKU number and price). She told me to leave them on the items. I repeated back to her three times that this would leave the price labels on the items even though they were gift wrapped. She said yes three times and was annoyed I kept asking her the same question. When she came to pick the gifts up, she screamed at me. Apparently, I was a moron for assuming she wanted the labels kept on the items. She kept at it. Caroline, the manager tried to calm the customer down but to no avail. Caroline ended up giving the lady her money back and I went into the manager's office and cried. Working in retail you see all sorts of bad behavior come out of seemingly nice people. Behavior I can laugh at in retrospect. I've had a customer throw a display sign at me and call me a "fucking bitch." Whatevs man. This lady got to me though and I don't know why. I love laughing at bad behavior, so if someone else had told me this story, I would've laughed heartily but because the bad behavior happened to me, I can't laugh. I see the irony.

Why was this retail bookstore with glorious customers the worst job I ever had? Well, to sum up, my coworkers. Every shift was like walking into the pits of hell full of evil minions who were there to destroy every fiber in my being. It's over now and that's the way it should be.

After struggling with my health, I managed to finish enough credits to apply to California State University Northridge (CSUN). Their film department is accomplished and well-regarded. I didn't get into the film production department. Instead I was put into the media criticism department. Everyone who gets into the media criticism department is someone who got into the film school at CSUN but just not into any of the other areas like production. I started taking classes and really enjoyed one.

The only class I enjoyed at CSUN was a film theory class and the professor was crazy in love with films and his enthusiasm. For him I tried, but didn't succeed, to show up to every session and I strove to write papers that were top quality. I got an A in that class. I took three classes that one semester and the film theory class was the only one I finished.

My film history class wasn't fun. The professor loved Orson Wells in a way no person should love Orson Wells. It was a sixteen-week semester and five weeks were dedicated to Orson Wells films. That's five films! I had no idea he made so many. The professor didn't even show Touch of Evil, which was Orson Wells's last film. Which blew my mind. Anyway, the final paper was suppose to be twenty pages and well, that was the end of my career as a film student at CSUN. A twenty page double spaced paper felt like too much of a challenge. I wanted to cry. Devastation was already running rampant in my life.

My mom had just passed away and there was little room in my brain to think straight. Not only did Mom passing destroy me emotionally, I let it cloud my judgement when it came to my school career. I had failed twice to get into CSUN's film production department but I was in the media criticism department. Had I just gotten my BA in media criticism, where would I have ended up? I might have gone on to teach film theory or film history or something awesome like that. I might have learned bigger and more awesome words other than "awesome."

After quitting CSUN, I went back to Pasadena City College to finish getting my AA. I took an Avid editing course. (Two software programs are used in the entertainment industry: Avid and Final Cut Pro. I already knew how to use Final Cut Pro.) The professor loved my work but as usual, I kept not showing up, so she refused to give me a work recommendation. Most of the time I missed class was due to grief over Mom. The professor had no sympathy for me. I realize most people go back to work shortly after a loved one dies, so her lack of sympathy is understandable. Plus, I was also starting to use Mom's death as an excuse to hide behind. I was having another episode. I simply have a hard time admitting when I have an episode. It's hard to confess my disorder to anyone.

I also repeated the course in which I was to make a 7-10 minute student film. Mine was about books, mental illness, and losing one's mother. At the beginning of the semester, we all put our desks in a circle and pitched our ideas to the class. When it was my turn one of the classmates said she didn't believe a woman over thirty would grieve for their mother. She was eighteen and just about everyone else yelled at her. It made me realize there really are two types of people in the world. The naive clueless ones and the ones that realize the world is bigger than they are. These two kinds of people come in any age.

I made Tinker Bell is Dead and though it's not as strong as a film as Hilary and Michael. It resonates with those who are in the sad club of having a dead mother. As a filmmaker, I couldn't ask for a better response in connecting with the audience the film was intended for.

In addition to jealousy, inspired is a feeling I don't like. Inspiration rarely leads to change. After graduating from college, I went to a seminar with a classmate, Steve, about making a web series. It was incredibly inspiring and I felt like I could pull off a web series. Steve and I made a pact to work together and get it done. Then we never talked to each other again. This pattern of feeling like you could accomplish anything and then waking up the next morning with the feeling gone isn't unique to my disorder. It happens all the time. I've only been truly lastingly inspired once and that was to write this book. It still took me over a year to finish a rough draft and it was rough. It's embarrassing but it gave me my start. Okay, I just admitted inspiration worked once for me but I basically avoid anything that bills itself as being inspirational.

Having a college degree was important to me. I simply didn't think it would happen. I earned my AA. Yes, it's only a two-year degree and it took me six years to get it, but get it I did. I can now say I'm a college graduate. Sure, it's easy for academic snots (and I have faced them) (also not everyone who is an academic is a snot) to look down at my AA but I'm going to quote Mark Twain again and say his philosophy on education is spot on. He once said, "I have never let my schooling interfere with my education." Okay, a quick Google search to get the exact quote informed me the quote can't be verified. Oh well. It's still a truthful quote and sounds like something he would say.

Chapter Nine

Goodnight Sweetheart

There are many things to help reinforce the bond and love between a mother and her child. Several moments in time can create something special. Something to remember or something to enjoy for only one day. These moments are as special and different for each mother and child. No two pairs are alike and this includes siblings. My sister's relationship with our mother was not the same as my relationship, and mine was not the same as my brother's.

My favorite moment with my mom was not a specific day but four separate nights during high school. If for any reason, it was just my mom and myself for the evening, we would open up a bottle of wine and slice up some cheese. Okay, I'll admit getting drunk with your teenage daughter sounds like bad parenting but it was who she was and we had several nights of fun. We called it "French Night" and got drunk and filled our bellies with yummy cheese. Our topics ranged from the hand cramps Jane Austen must have had from handwriting so many novels (though not as many novels as Charles Dickens, so his hands probably hurt more, we concluded) to my future as a brilliant film director. After I made my first million, I was to promptly buy her a big house and a Jaguar. Jane Austen would have written more books if only her hand didn't hurt so much (well, it didn't help that Jane was 41 when she died) and I would change the world through film.

Mom was such a force of positive energy that it's not easy to remember she also had a dark side. Not dark, like evil, but more of an intensely crazy selfish side. She was to my best assessment bipolar and not medicated. The medications at the time were not as helpful as they are now. It didn't help that she fell victim to the thought that is common among mentally ill people. The thought is after starting to feel better a few weeks into her treatment plan, she could stop taking the medication because her mental state had improved. I kept telling Mom she felt better because of her medication and not in spite of it. Would she have been capable of taking the better medicine that is on the market today with that attitude? The answer is painfully no. One belief she held and would tell me often was that this is how God designed her (and me) and she shouldn't alter how God wanted her to spend her life.

It didn't matter to me that she rejected my commitment to medication and psychiatrists. I continued to fight for an average life. A life without a mental illness running rampant in my head. On more than one occasion she told me I was wonderful and beautiful just as I am. It would have been nice if she would have been supportive but this was one of the few issues where we disagreed. During the time the two of us spent with each other, we never fought. She did completely understand my aversion to yelling and never raised her voice.

Mom firmly believed in reincarnation and she had a vision once of her being my mother in a past life. We lived in Ireland in the eighteenth century. This is where Mom's obsession that I was Irish came from. I grew up honestly believing her mom was Irish because that's what Mom told me. It wasn't until after Mom's passing that her sisters shared with me that Irish isn't in my blood. No one knew why Mom kept insisting I was Irish, but a few years after her passing, I started to remember all the times Mom told me she was my mother before this life. It all made sense. Mom was full of mischief and half truths. This was just one of them. Unless, of course, reincarnation is real and Mom was correct for all those years.

When we moved into our house in San Jose, McDonalds had a special drink called the Coke Float. It's a root beer float but with Coke instead. McDonalds was also giving away with each Coke Float purchase a souvenir Coke Float glass cup. Mom and I spent the first week or so fixing up the house we had rented and when we needed to take a food break, we went to McDonalds and ordered that special drink. I don't really like cola all that much but it was nice sharing the Coke Float experience with her. By the time we were ready to move in, we had a collection of twenty-two glasses. They didn't survive for long as they were made from cheap glass and easily broke. However, the memories of that time spent with her are unforgettable.

One of my strongest memories of Mom is how much she loved to garden. She had a green thumb and she claimed it was relaxing. I don't share the same passion for flowers and vegetables and she never asked for much help. She did say she wanted me to keep her company and that I did. I miss conversing with Mom. I miss the years of conversations I should have had with her. She passed halfway through a life span and there are times I really could use her advice, one of her jokes, or to simply hear her voice.

Every now and again, Mom would come into my room at bedtime and ask me if I wanted to run away with her the next day. Running away with Mom was the best. We would wake up before the sun rose and drive off into a little adventure. She always found quaint little cafes to go for breakfast and then, more often than not, we would go into the mountains for a hike. Mom was a photographer and she loved photographing nature. Somehow I wound up holding all the camera equipment but I never once minded. When we moved to western Washington, we started to take hikes in the rainforest (What?!? There's a rainforest in the States? You bet there is. Did I just blow your mind? Unless, of course, you already knew that. Then I bet you're rolling your eyes). I loved running away with Mom and having a few precious alone hours with her. I knew way back then I would always cherish the memories of our mornings together.

I have anxiety about waiting for someone to pick me up because of her. She would often forget to pick me up. Shortly after starting the second small-town high school, Mom said she would pick me up after school so I wouldn't have to take the bus. School was let out and the buses all left. In fact the parking lot emptied out and Mom was nowhere to be found. I tried to call the house but the phone lines were down. Since I was new to town. I had yet to learn how to walk to my house that was 14 miles from the school. Mom hadn't had time to take us shopping for winter clothes and thus I had nothing warm on. Through the window of the principal's office there was a big red digital clock. The hours kept passing by. A few people asked me if I wanted a ride home and I turned them all down. I didn't want Mom to freak out when she came to get me and I wasn't there. Afternoon turned into evening which turned into night. The school became deserted as everyone went home for the evening. I didn't know anyone and I still had a big city mentality. A teenage girl should never ring the doorbell of a stranger in the dark hours of the day. Night in turn became midnight I envisioned the school starting a new day by finding a frozen Meaghan outside the building. At 12:30 am, Pop showed up. Mom had completely forgotten me. Pop only realized where I was when he got home at midnight and found me not asleep in my bed. He woke up Mom and she said something along the lines that I must have been at school. Mom never apologized for leaving me there. It's not like she was unfeeling but Mom was in denial about her illness and refused to acknowledge any hiccups in her behavior. I love my mom but well now, I always have back up plans when someone says they'll pick me up.

The worst day of my life was not when my mom passed away, but three months before when she called to tell me that the cancer had spread. It was then that it fully hit me, the time my mother had on Earth was not only finite but ending sooner than it should have been. She was only fifty-four. This could not truly be the end. How could it be? Yes, I had been out of the house for a decade but she was still needed. Mom knew I loved her and I know she loved me. She's gone but there's not a doubt in my mind of the strong relationship we had. It's preposterous that she passed away at all and inconceivable that my sons (I'll get to them) will never know their grandmother and yet it's a fact.

The last time I saw Mom was shortly after she said the cancer had spread. I went up to help her with her funeral arrangements. Leaving her to go home was one of the hardest things I've ever done. When it was time to leave, I went to give Mom a hug and a kiss and to say, for what would be the last time, "good-bye." I wanted to look her in the eyes one last time and smile and let her know how greatly I love her. However, Mom was in a deep sleep because of all her painkillers. I couldn't stir her at all. Trust me I tried. It got to the point if I stayed any longer I would miss my flight. The thought of missing my flight crossed my mind, but I needed to get home. I left with my final moments of Mom being me crying because I couldn't wake her up. I cried a cry that could only have been comforted by my mom but if Mom had been able to give me a hug, I wouldn't have needed the comfort. It was a Catch-22 that I still can't wrap my mind around.

Two months later, Pop called and told me Mom was convinced I was mad at her. Pop put Mom on the phone and Mom was crying asking me why I was mad at her. I started to cry and I told her there is no way I'd ever be mad at her. Not in a million years. She was my perfect mother and I wouldn't want anyone else. She calmed down and then Pop got on the phone and said Mom had fallen asleep.

The day she died, Pop called me to say that Mom was dying and it was time to say "goodbye." This was the first and thus far the only time I heard the labored breathing of someone about to pass. I told her I loved her and she was an amazing light in my life. I began to cry and couldn't get any further words out. Pop came back on the phone and told me he needed to call my brother. I hung up and an hour later, Pop called back to tell me Mom was gone.

She had pancreatic cancer. I had known for fifteen months this was going to be the end result but nothing could prepare me for the how brutal it would feel to have my heart ripped out of my chest. I still can't think of last moments of her life without crying. I'm crying right now and cry about it when I dwell on it. There is never getting over the loss of a mother. There are days when the pain is raw just as it was the day she died. There is moving past but no getting over. I try to remember her when she was healthy and full of life and not the broken and beat up person she became because of cancer treatments.

Growing up, we would sing 'Goodnight, Sweetheart' to each other every night at bedtime. This was such a tradition that it was kept up even after I moved out of the house. We didn't call each other up on the phone to sing 'Goodnight, Sweetheart' every night but every time I visited, we picked up right where we left off. After her funeral and before the reception, the service room emptied out. I took the opportunity to walk up to her coffin and sing the song to her one last time. I just couldn't believe she was gone. It made no sense that I was left all in this world without her. I was twenty-eight but I still needed my mommy. I find that I sing the song to my boys at bedtime now. It's not a conscience decision, it's just something that naturally comes out of my mouth. It helps heal the pain of her loss.

For the first time in my life I experienced true depression. Losing Mom made me realize how hollow all my depressive episodes are. The pain was real and not only in my mind. It was interesting to feel depression on such a high level. I know what it's like to be normal sad. I know normal grief. Even though I still have depressed episodes, I'm able to pull out a mental ruler and measure the episode to the pain of losing Mom. Is this episode as deep as Mom's death? Not once has the answer been "yes" and the fact makes episodes of depression even easier to get past.

Everyone paints the world with their own colors. When someone dies, their colors are also lost. My mom's were lost on April 21, 2008. Several years later during my son Theodore's first Halloween at school, my in-laws were there to watch him as he trick-or-treated throughout the campus. My in-laws were having a good time as I sat on a bench, miserable and pregnant. I looked at them and thought, "We should make copies of the pictures to send to Mom." With that thought and the moment of temporary forgetfulness, the world once again had my mom's colors in it. For that split second, all was right and happy. Then like a sucker punch to the heart, I remembered that she was no longer alive. My world suddenly seemed like an awful shade of gray. It was everything I could do to not sob uncontrollably. I wanted to lose myself in the raw emotion of knowing she's gone. Instead, I lifted my head to face the world again and saw my son's enjoyment screaming "trick-or-treat!" I saw the world with his color palette and took comfort in it.

My mother. I love her, I love her, I love her. She was the perfect mother for me. Love does not fade away with death. I love her a great deal and until I breathe my last breath, my love for her will be present tense.

Chapter Ten

The Music Goes Round My Head

June, 2009 was the start of my first grossly exaggerated belief or in other words a grand delusion. Once an idea is planted in me, it's hard to pull me out of the fantasy world I now live in. Any delusion makes it nearly impossible to tell the difference between reality and what is imagined. The made up story that started my decent into schizophrenia started a year after my mom's passing. But it would take three years before I could even admit schizophrenia was now something else I lived with. What narrative did my brain invent for me? Hold on, here we go.

My mother came to me in a dream and told me my biological father was someone else. I woke up and took this dream as truth. Now, just to be clear, I look a lot like my dad. We had the same blond hair as a child, brown hair later in life, and the same color blue eyes. This is not enough for you? Well, schizophrenia runs rampant on my dad's side of the family tree. This may not seem like much but it's all I have to hold on to. Even though my episode is over, it lays in the back of my mind as a possible truth.

I talked to as many people as I could about my dream. Oh, and I failed to mention it was a dream. Of course, I didn't tell my father. If I did, then I'd have to face the fact that I was on a good case of being a lunatic. I also didn't want my father to know because of the pain it would inflict on him. He may not be father of the year but he is the only biological father I have. Him knowing that I was running around claiming not to belong to him would have devastated him. However, I did contemplate getting ahold of his DNA, so I could do a test that would prove my theory. Whenever he visited and stayed the night, I would search the bathroom high and low for a usable piece of hair. I never found one. It's as thought Dad knew what I was up to and would scrub the bathroom clean when he came to stay the night. Now, Mom's need to paint me as Irish made complete sense. I must have been someone else's daughter. A man who was Irish. Who knows. Maybe said Irish dude is my father. It took me a while to remember Mom's past life fantasy that I was her daughter hundreds of years ago and we lived in Ireland. A much better explanation than my biological father was an Irishman. That's what I continue to tell myself.

One of the people I talked to was Mom's younger sister. She said Mom would have told her if I wasn't my father's biological daughter. Even with that, I was still skeptical.

It's hard to imagine I'm part of Dad because we are so different. I'm very much my mother's daughter. This was my brain's way of coping. The delusional episode has ended and I have, for the most part, come to terms with my linage.

Here's another bad transition: One good thing that came from Mom passing away was I finally got to know my cousin, Sean, and all of his awesomeness. A month after Mom passed, my step-grandmother made her way to Heaven. Pop flew down from Washington state to for the memorial service and Mom's two sisters and Sean picked Pop and me up for the three hour trip to San Luis Obispo. As Sean and I started to talk and started to click, I became very mad at our parents for not being closer to each other. If they had, I would have had Sean in my life since my childhood. He quickly became one of my core friends.

Sean lived two hours away but he worked twenty minutes from my house. I would meet him for lunch about once a week. Sometimes we would meet for dinner on Friday nights and have a blast. I looked forward to that one hour a week we shared a meal. Neither one of us celebrate

Valentine's Day with our significant other, so we thought nothing of going to dinner on that holiday. Our waitress kept winking at us and giving a knowing smile. No amount of protest made the waitress believe we weren't on a date. Finally Sean blurted out that we don't live in Alabama. Sean and I look a lot a like and have a lot of the same mannerisms. We're definitely related, without a shred of gray area. I laughed very hard and to this day believe the waitress thought we were having an affair. That's what I get for having a male friend. See Sean and I have the same way of thinking. We can speak half sentences to each other and completely get what the other one means.

After graduating from college, I decided to have a tonsillectomy to take care of my gnarly tonsils and also have my deviated septum fixed. My nose and throat surgery was a long time coming. The whole procedure was painful and you don't get to eat all the ice cream you want after all because you can't eat anything cold. Not at first. I lived on room temperature ramen noodles. It's as nasty as it sounds. Anyway, the story here isn't my surgery, it's what happened when I developed a sinus infection two weeks post surgery and the surgeon gave me a steroid to knock out the infection. I always read the paperwork the pharmacy gives me with my prescriptions. The warning label said to not take the steroid if you take a mood stabilizer. This was on Thursday. I called my psychiatrist and left a message. Friday came and no response from my doctor. I'd just had nose surgery and the infection was causing a bunch of pain. I took a chance and started the steroid. Holy crap. That was a bad idea. Almost immediately, the power of my medications were eradicated. Auditory hallucinations kicked in and mania then depression then mania then depression then mania again and then back to depression all within the matter of moments gave me mental whiplash. I yelled at my doctor in my yelling voice (which is actually not a yell at all, just polite frustration) when he called me on Monday to tell me not to take the steroid because it would have a negative impact on my medication. It took me four months to recover.

While recovering, I got a job offer to direct a short film. I jumped at the chance, even though I wasn't well. The script was not well written and the producer was a flake but it was a job. For once it wasn't my illness that was my downfall. In fact it had nothing to do with me. The producer was late to every meeting except one. For that one she stood me up. I quit on her. I don't like showing up either but she crossed a line by not informing me that she would be late or not coming at all. It's hard to work with someone who won't be there. Yes, I'm aware of the irony.

The grand delusion that my father wasn't my biological father lasted two years. In the meantime, I had at least five bipolar episodes starting with the one caused by steroids. The grand delusion was a whole new sensation. I somehow managed to simultaneously be in denial about having schizophrenia and fully accept being bipolar with psychotic tendencies. While having the delusion there was also a little bit of mania every time I talked to someone about it. Since most of my episodes are mixed, having added mania really made my brain ache. Physically ache. My brain literally hurt. Why this didn't raise any red flags about my diagnoses changing I'll never know. I don't blame anyone but me for not noticing. I never told my doctor or therapist about my dead mother telling me some other man was my biological father. I may have been going crazy, but I wasn't stupid. As much as I believed the lie with all my heart, my brain knew it was a lie. To get this all straight, let's recap (even thought I just started on this subject a few paragraphs before): I believed my father wasn't my father even though buried deep in my brain I knew it wasn't true and I was still having bipolar mixed episodes. No wonder my brain was throbbing. The symptoms of my illness were becoming worse.

In 2011, I started to calm down regarding my grand delusion. There wasn't a moment where I suddenly accepted my lineage. It was more of a gradual end. I justified my beliefs by thinking I was just manic for two years. I was truly ashamed by my thoughts and actions but I didn't correct myself to anyone. I never apologized. I never went around and told my friends the truth. This was another example of me not wanting to look like a raving lunatic, so I kept my mouth shut. I didn't really understand what happened and it seemed there was no way to explain it.

I imagine I'm slightly unbearable to deal with. My mind freaks out at a moment's notice. My brain is hard to live with and I should know. I live with it. However, the average stranger has no idea about my condition. Mental illness can't be seen. From the outside looking in, I appear to be perfectly normal. I seem to be an average person. However, I'm prone to paranoia and mania. Depression and elation. Schizophrenia and hallucinations. Sometimes I can't tell I'm not myself because I'm always me. The chaos in my head can be hard to cover up, even in the simplest of situations.

My friends all know about my condition. I have to tell them. At least at some point, to explain my behavior. I don't have a lot of friends because I don't want to keep explaining myself when I act out of the ordinary. Seeming like a normal human with a normal human mind is something to strive for. I try and try but when my illness gets the better of me, I just have to move on. I have to let the interaction go. In a brief lapse of my masquerade, I let the world see my mental state for what it truly is: a bunch of messy noise that rarely is logical and even more rarely makes sense. My illness doesn't make sense. There's some science trying to explain why my brain ticks the way it does but that science doesn't make a lick of difference until there is a cure. What would I do without my illness? It's a part of me and all I know.

In 2010, Jonathan and I celebrated our ten-year anniversary and we did so by heading up to wine country.

Now, I'm not suppose to drink more than five alcoholic drinks a month because alcohol reduces the effectiveness of my medication. Well, in the one week of our vacation, I became fast and loose with the five drinks a month rule and had seven drinks. I wanted to live in a world where I didn't have a disorder and could drink as much as I wanted. I just wanted to be normal, if only for a little bit. It took me four weeks to recover from the semi-massive mixed episode that came on. The anxiety of missing work and basically not feeling well made my doctor prescribe Xanax to be taken everyday for two weeks. That was a great helper. It worked better than taking my gold standard, Ativan. That would be the only time I took Xanax and the last time I drank that much. I love alcohol but I love being stable even more.

One of the managers that interviewed me at the fifth Barnes and Noble I worked at was Miranda. Neither of us knew at the time that we would become friends. We talked a bit and she seemed to like me a lot but I was being a big pooper which, let's face it, I normally am. Shortly after I started, she moved away. Once she was gone, I realized how much I wanted to be friends with her. Then a few months after moving away, the Heavens opened up and I got a second chance at friendship. Miranda moved back and was rehired at Barnes and Noble. Why all mushy bits when it comes to Miranda? What can I say, I love Miranda. Miranda's awesome and I'm quite sure that's all she'll let me write about her.

I actually don't know why the Thousand Oaks Barnes and Noble didn't fire me. I ran a fine line of insubordination when it came to selling Nooks (the company's e-reader). I told one of the assistant managers what a hard time I have selling the Nook and I didn't think I had it in me to sell people an electronic device. She explained to me that she puts on an act every time she clocks in. She's herself until she clocks in and then she can put on an act in which she's a Nook selling machine. I almost screamed, "I do put on an act! I got up, smelled my clothes, pick the least offensive one, ate some breath mints, styled my hair to hide how dirty it was, and drove to work! I'm here and that's my act!" Instead I thanked her for the advice and walked away. I probably should have been written up.

In my thirtieth year on this planet my brain became worse. I had gotten so comfortable in the rhythm of a bipolar mind that even though schizophrenia was a possibility (because of, you guessed it, my dad's family tree), I wouldn't admit that my diagnosis had evolved into another level of seriousness. I ignored the warning sign via the "Dad isn't my father" delusion. It took another two and a half years before I was able to disclose to myself I had a problem. I was bipolar with psychotic tendencies. That is what I knew and that is all I wanted to know. A few months before I was able to come to the conclusion that something was terribly wrong, I stopped taking my medicine. I actually halted my drug intake. This is something I didn't realize I was doing and it took Jonathan noticing my pill bottles weren't emptying as quickly as usual to discover my self-sabotage.

I was living in a mental state I hadn't felt before. This is yet another period of time where I almost have no memory. I just knew something had changed. I started researching if it was possible to be bipolar and schizophrenic and I found a useful term to bring to my psychiatrist: Schizoaffective disorder. Schizoaffective disorder is schizophrenia and bipolar. There was what I was living with put succinctly.

In January of 2012, a friend got me a job as the head craft services (craft services = food for the film crew) person for a music video. The shoot was two days and seventeen hours both days. The set was a two-hour drive from my house. I made it through the shoot but I collapsed after getting home the second day. I couldn't get out of bed for three days. This was the first time I paid attention to how the stress of the entertainment industry wasn't something I could cope with. My disorder made complete focus and actually showing up on an everyday basis something I couldn't achieve. I tried to ignore the warning that film making isn't something I can handle, there was doubt. Going against this knowledge, I tried to make a short film.

Writing the screenplay for the short wasn't really any trouble but getting it made was an uphill challenge that I lost. I needed about $5000 to make the short and someone suggested I do a Kickstarter campaign. I raised $300. Then there was the nightmare of trying to find a location. I could use my house for most of the scenes but I needed a restaurant and I went to two local restaurants where I was a regular. One manager screamed a "no" at me. At the second restaurant, the manager told me he'd send me an email with the answer after he spoke with his wife and he never bothered to respond to my inquiry. I put out an ad for actors and most of the actors flaked on even showing up for the audition. Finally, I had a cast in place and then one of the actors dropped out at the last minute. Finding a camera man also proved to be nearly impossible. I did find a camera man and he actually offered me a job after the production of my short fell through but the offer came too late. It was too depressing to carry on. After years of dreaming and two short student films and countless attempts at being someone who could actually make a full length feature film I threw in the towel. Not only could I not handle the stress, I'm an awkward person and the number of people I would've had to deal with while making a film was too daunting.

In the time between the grand delusion and being diagnosed with schizoaffective disorder, I had started to have deep paranoia issues. No longer was the paranoia cute and easy to handle. I started to believe everyone was out to kill me. Walking into any shopping store became a struggle for fear a gunman would come into the store and shoot everyone. It took a lot of will power to walk into a store. If a driver was tailgating me or driving behind me for a couple of turns, I believed the driver wanted me dead. I would drive erratically and then pull into a parking lot just so the driver could pass. This level of paranoia was something new and I didn't know how to handle it. When I finally confessed to my doctor what my brain was doing and my illness had advanced, my brain was in bad shape. My brain hurt from living in lies and fighting a new level of psychosis. The experiment to find the right combination of medication began. Again.

Just as that started, I became pregnant and couldn't take anything because the super strong meds weren't good for my baby. It would be another year before I was able to get back to finding the drugs that worked for me.

After the new diagnosis, I took a leave of absence from the bookstore. Since I wan't classified as an employee with benefits, I just talked to my manager and she agreed to let me take the time I needed and to come back for the holiday season. The holiday season was six months away. I thought six months would give me a chance to acclimation to the new brain lifestyle. Also, who knew how long it would take to find a good combo of medication? Six months may not have been enough time for both acclamation and a good medication regimen to happen but it was a good start. I needed to start somewhere. However, after two and half years of trying and failing to get pregnant, I gave up. Mainly because of my new upgraded diagnoses.

Of course, as soon as I gave up, I became pregnant.

Now, back to the too late job offer from the camera man. He offered me a job as assistant director the day after I found out I was pregnant. My psychiatrist told me I needed a stress-free pregnancy and my obstetrician agreed. Thus ending both my retail career and my dreams of being a film director. I was all too happy to leave the bookstore but it took a while to move forward from my lifelong dream of being a filmmaker. I used my pregnancy as an excuse to turn down the cameraman's job but really, my brain couldn't handle the pressure of long crazy hours. The disappointment of not being able to make my short was more than I could handle. That and I'm better in solitude work-wise and I finally accepted that fact.

Chapter Eleven

I Am Not a Robot

It's interesting living with two disorders that are opposites on the emotional scale. Bipolar is a very emotional disorder. The rapid change between manic and depressive is a wonder to behold but it is mainly about feelings. I felt depressed, manic, or both. I felt like my soul was being ripped in two. I felt with all my heart all the feeling on the spectrum of feelings. But with schizophrenia, I felt nothing. Nothing at all. I was becoming robotic with feelings buried inside me with no way to get out. If my face is blank, don't assume I'm unfeeling. Just because I don't have the appropriate response doesn't mean I'm not empathizing. There is a clear difference between how I behaved with only the bipolar disorder and how I became after the schizophrenia took ahold of me.

One of the frustrating aspects of schizophrenia is believing lies. Lies I tell myself, or imagine to be real. It takes a concerted effort to not fall into the world of paranoia and to make something up and then swear it's true. When I do make something up, normally to impress someone, I call it "Meaghan Facts." The little stories I create can mask as something that kind of sounds like it's true.

I have learned to reply slowly when being asked a question because if I don't think it through, I'll make something up and call it a day. Making something up, tends to falls into the category of letting shit fall out of my mouth. The last sentence is the only and best way to describe what happens. Stupid shit that makes me look stupid. There is no longer a fast conversation with me. If I'm talking quickly, then

I'm more likely than not making something up. Then there's a kicker- I believe the lie with all my heart, my whole body, and mind. It horrifies me because I know it isn't true but can't stop from believing it. It's something I can't control well. I can just try to rein it in. After shit falls out of my mouth, I try to immediately apologize and say the truth. Sometimes it takes me a few hours to be able to come around and admit to the Meaghan Fact. Admit I just lied. If I don't know you well, and don't feel like explaining the Meaghan Fact then I let it go and move on.

My sons' poor pediatrician. He dealt with me during postpartum psychosis and postpartum mania. Theodore's head was really big as an infant and when the doctor asked me if any family member has a large head, I answered that my husband does. Never mind the fact that Jonathan's helmet size is medium. I went on to talk about Jonathan's big head. Oh well.

I can also lie to your face. Lying to a customer's face was something I did all the time. Even at the fifth (and last) Barnes and Noble I worked at (in Thousand Oaks in 2009), I was talking to a coworker about an actress/singer and said that I liked her acting but not her singing. A customer walked in and picked up the actress's album and I exclaimed how much I love her singing. My coworker looked horrified.

For some more bookselling fun stories, I shall now share two that happened during my tenure at the Thousand Oaks Barnes and Noble. My two favorite young adult books to sell were the book series The Bloody Jack Adventures and anything by the author Mary Hooper. I can't choose between the two as one of my customers can attest to. She asked me to recommend a book for her thirteen-year-old niece and I gave her Newes From the Dead by Mary Hooper and the first book in the Bloody Jack adventures. She asked me to choose the better one and I couldn't and she ended up buying another book from a display. I still can't tell you which one is better because L.A. Meyer (author of the Bloody Jack series) and Mary Hooper are both amazing authors. I tear my hair out even thinking about it, so I'm going to stop.

In 2010, I had a lady throw a tantrum in the middle of the children's department. Yes, a full-on tantrum usually seen from a two-year-old. She laid down on the floor and everything. Why? Someone had put back all the books she had put on hold the day before and she couldn't remember what she had picked. The books were set to be gifts and she didn't have time to pick out books again. I kind of thought she was being silly at the time and more than slightly immature. Then the MacGruber incident happened.

I went to visit my sister and Pop a year after my mom passed away and it was a week not to be remembered for its lightheartedness. Seeing all Mom's stuff basically as it she left it was draining. I spent the whole week going through Mom's massive pile of belongings. I bought the hilarious movie MacGruber on Blu-ray (Meaghan Fact- I'm the only person who likes this film) while there. My plan was to go home and watch all of the following in one day, MacGruber, Cannibal the Musical, and Blades of Glory. In that order. Well, the movie fest day came and I put in MacGruber and it wouldn't play. I went to Target and purchased their last copy on Blu-ray. That copy didn't play either. It must have been my Blu-ray player but I couldn't figure out why. It had all its current updates and other discs played just fine when tried. I just wanted my hilarious movie day to wipe away the memory of the previous week. I drove back to Target because the day had to start with MacGruber. That's how my brain put in the order of the films and that's how it needed to go. The nice manager told me he couldn't take back the Blu-ray because it was open and he could only exchange it for another Blu-ray. I know how the policy worked. It's just they didn't have another copy. I nearly had a tantrum right there and then. I suddenly understood the lady who laid down on the pee-stained children's department floor and cried. I almost cried. I did convince the manager to let me exchange the Blu-ray for the DVD and I went home and had my marathon. I really felt for the poor employees, I've been in their shoes. I know what it's like to deal with a customer who behaved as I had.

There has been more than one person in my life who has called me out when the pile of stinky poo comes out of my mouth and I get frustrated because my mind is stuck on the untruth and my brain freezes in horror. I have to retrain my mind to the truth. It's embarrassing but taking the time to breathe and let go of the lies does stop the train so I can concentrate on what I'm saying, for a while anyway. I always start to forget the lesson and begin to pull stuff out of my ass again. One of the situations that sticks out in my mind, because it's one of the few that's not traumatizing to reflect on, was a conversation I had with my friend, Amber, about Veronica Mars. We had seen the movie a few weeks back and man alive, I was creating stories. Stories about the success of the film and if it's going to turn back into a TV show. She calmly shut me down. I was horrified because I really like Amber and instead of impressing her with Meaghan Facts, I looked like an idiot.

When I tell people about my disorder, the main comment I get is "you seem normal." I'll tell you something-after several years of living with a mental illness, I became an expert on seeming. I realized early on that any mental illness was generally met with a lack of understanding and a propensity to willfully think said person with the illness is making it up. I have heard often enough that my illness is all in my mind. Of course it's in my mind. That is literally what I just said. Thinking I'm making up my illness is a load of crap but it's impossible to get the stupid idiot to change their mind. Saying the term "stupid idiot" sounds harsh so let me soften it up for you. Ignorant person. Is that better? Ignorant people can become difficult to handle because most of them want to live in their ignorance and not learn to have an open mind and heart about my disorder. I'm a little combative when it comes to opening up about my illness. I have lost a lot of respect for people I respected because they then saw me as weak.

Seeming normal is difficult but it's something I've been practicing since I was sixteen years old. In high school, I opened up a little to some friends and the reaction wasn't good. Those friends' reactions made me realize I can't go through life showing everyone my illness. It became something to hide and now I have to pretend nothing is wrong. No one would suspect this, because I'm a really good actor. I put my game face on every time I walk out the door. By the time I graduated from high school, I had mastered the art of seeming. When the fog rolls in and I begin to drown in a sea of lunacy, I pretend nothing is wrong. It takes energy away from my mental situation, so my episodes take a bit longer to get over. Mom didn't do me any favors when she taught me in high school that sick days come first. I almost had to repeat the eleventh grade because of a terrible episode and she let me stay home to rest. I learned it was okay to take the time I needed to feel better. The real world doesn't work that way. It works on people having perfect attendance and working while under the weather. I called in sick to have rest days for my brain. Then when I was at work, I played an Academy Award winning role. Unfortunately (or fortunately, depending how you look at it), no one knew I was putting on a performance for everyone's benefit. At least though, I still had my feelings and my animated facial expressions.

As the schizophrenia took ahold of me, my feelings became more and more buried where I couldn't find them. This horrifying new reality also came with my face becoming more and more stone-like. And so did my heart. Not only was I losing my emotions, I was losing the ability to show emotions even when I had them. People would begin to realize I wan't normal. As a society, our facial expressions are an important way to communicate. It was one thing for me to not feel much, it was another thing to not be able to hide who I really am.

The stone face was especially hard for me to deal with. I have always been known for my wonderful facial expressions. As a child, teen, and young adult, people would exclaim how they loved my facial expressions. Those days are long gone.

To cope, I began to practice facial expressions in the mirror and taught myself how each expression looks and feels. A smile is this way, concerned is like that, so on and so forth. It took a lot of practice and to this day, I still give myself brush up lessons. There are times, when I realized too late that the wrong expression is (or was) on my face. Someone can tell me a sad story and I accidentally smile. "What I'm saying isn't funny." Crapity crapity crap crap crap. Oh well.

I've also had to come up with a list of small talk responses because small talk happens almost everyday. I've learned that when someone asks how you're doing, the best way to respond is to say "Well, thank you" and not "Okay."

I love being okay. When people said, "Just okay?" I would say, "Okay is good enough for me." They had no idea about my illness and I was just telling the truth. I've since learned that most people don't want to hear anything less than a completely positive reply, so now I smile and just say, "Well, thank you."

The whole being robotic with no emotions thing finally got to me. It took some time, as my main schizophrenic symptom was extreme paranoia. When it happened, it really happened. I went from being overly emotional to having no facial expressions and a cold heart. There had been plenty of love for friends and family but the love in my heart puttered out. It was scary.

About five months after my diagnosis, I became pregnant. At the first ultrasound, I cried tears of joy and fell in love. I love my child and that's how I knew I wasn't completely dead inside.

Also after giving birth, I started to take Latuda, a new to the market anti-psychotic, and my heart is better. Facial expression are still difficult and I can still be cold-hearted but it is nothing compared to how I was before taking the anti-psychotic.

Never with my sons do I have to think about which facial expression I need. My face moves on its own. Not as well as it did but enough to make me sigh a breath of relief because my boys should always know how much I love them.

Still, when I'm tired it's hard to muster up the energy to move my face. It's really draining seeming all day long. By the time evening rolls around I just want to be left alone with my stone face. Sure, it's easier to move my face around my boys but I do get tired. There will come a day when the boys will know about my condition. I hope that they will realize that this is part of who I am and not how I feel about them.

I am always either going into an episode, in the middle of an episode, or coming out of one. If I'm lucky I may have a few days of rest in between, but I know I'll always dragged back into one. The added bit of schizophrenia just means the I experience a wider variety of episodes now. Bipolar disorder gives me depressed, manic, and mixed episodes. Psychotic tendencies episodes, where I often hear voices, are added into the mix of bipolar episodes. Fun fun. Schizophrenia gives me extreme paranoia. The auditory hallucinations can be added to the paranoia. Sometimes with visual hallucinations as well. Doubled the fun. Paranoia can also show up during a mix with any bipolar episode. Extra fun. Then there are the visual hallucinations. Fun galore. When things become very bad, I call my doctor and my meds are adjusted.

I love my medication. My psych meds are some of my friends. It's a little tedious to work with medication but it's well worth it. Episodes aren't as bad as they used to be. It helps there are better medications on the market, though not all medications are wonder drugs. I have had some bad reactions to medications. It takes perseverance to find the right combination of medications. It took me ten years to finally have the balance I sought. Yes, I just said a decade.

As a child, when I figured out not everyone had the same mental issues, one of my tools to help me get through the days was hope. Hope that I would one day be not as sick as I was. I felt with every fiber of my being there would be a day things wouldn't be so bad. I didn't think it would come in pill form but when I had the life-altering episode all those years ago. I accepted medication was the way to go.

Chapter Twelve

The One No One Thought About

Every woman has a battle story when it comes to pregnancy and/or labor.

My pregnancy with Theodore was mainly uneventful. Sure, I peed every ten to fifteen minutes, causing me to not get much sleep throughout my pregnancy, was diagnosed with gestational diabetes, and had bronchitis the last five weeks of the pregnancy but that it all seemed like run of the mill pregnancy crap.

My battle moment came with labor. I was in labor for eighteen hours after which I had an emergency C-section. I won't bore you with any more of my labor story than this paragraph and this paragraph is ending now.

With my mental illness, my psychiatrist naturally assumed I'd develop postpartum depression. But after Theodore was born on a rainy day in January, I wanted to wait on taking my medication because I wanted to breastfeed. It was three weeks before I found myself hiding in the closet holding Theodore because that was the only place the government couldn't find us. I was holding Theodore tight and rocking back and forth when I realized something was wrong with my mental state. This felt like a new level of delusion, even for me. I was in the grip of full-blown postpartum psychosis.

My paranoia didn't stop with the government. The fear of someone taking an automatic rifle to the store where I was shopping was worse. Even the driver-out-to-get-me one became so bad that I limited the amount of times I drove.

The gunman at the store was tricky. I had to battle this delusion with my insane urge to spend money.

What would win out? The need to shop, the drivers, or a bullet-filled trip to the store of my choice? It was an epic struggle. If I didn't leave the house, I shopped online. If I left the house, I spent more money for instant gratification.

Strangers became my enemy too. Innocent-looking strangers. Strangers that just wanted to connect with a woman and her new baby. I tried to avoid these interactions as much as possible. It's hard though because a lot of people want to look at newborns. Babies are the future of this world and give hope to many. I was living in my head and became irrationally offended by many of the nice comments Theodore would get. One woman said all lovingly that Theodore was a new baby. I became mad and informed her that Theodore was not new. In fact he turned ten weeks old that day. The woman looked confused and shocked as I huffed off.

A short gallop through racing thoughts is now in order. An unexpectedly damaging aspect of my condition was how fast my thoughts raced. I had experienced racing thoughts before, and had managed to control this symptom. But now it was a speed I never thought possible. Being able to control my thoughts is something I pride myself on. The neck braking pace proved to be too much. My thoughts went a little like this:

howareyouImgreatthankyouitsgoodtoseeyouandourvisittod
ayshouldbefunIreallyenjoyseeingyouandthisisreallyatreatThe
odoreisjustfineheiseatingwellandsleepingthroughthenightyea
hweredoingreat.

My mouth couldn't keep up with the speed of my brain. My actual speech went something like this:

"How are you? I'm great. Good to see you. Today fun. The great."

It was so bad that I stopped talking. I could barely function speech wise.

As the psychosis started to ease up, I had to retrain myself to talk. Theodore first birthday was when I started to be able to communicate in a normal fashion. When Theodore turned ten months old, I realized he needed to get out of the house more often. Story time at the library seemed like a good activity to do and I sucked up my aversion to the pain of libraries. We started going. I was still having difficulty speaking and being around other parents was not easy. Talking to strangers has never been a strong suit of mine and not being able to explain exactly why I was basically mute made spending time with other mothers terrible. After about five weeks I decided to stop going. The stress of participating was too great.

The paranoia I felt wasn't limited to the government, gunmen, or homicidal maniac drivers. I started to believe my loved ones were out to get me. Well, not get me but hated me. It caused me to become a little standoffish to those who loved me and I couldn't see past my paranoia to correctly explain to them what was truly going on. For the most part, I kept my thoughts to myself. Okay, I couldn't really talk as it was because of my lightening speed racing mind so it was easier to just live in my head. For around a year I cut myself off from friends and family. And then it passed.

One really great symptom of postpartum psychosis is an inability to sleep. I was able to keep the hours that Theodore kept and more. He normally woke up at 3:30 am hungry and I would feed him and then lie awake watching TV on my phone and wait for the sun to rise. Then at 6:30 am, I'd take Theodore for an hour's walk in the stroller while he slept. I was also hyper enough to go on a few walks a day. I was able to lose my baby weight in nine months because of this ability to be awake and energetic almost all the time.

Outdoor walks around my neighborhood weren't stress-free. On every walk I feared that we would be mugged and/or shot. But that fear wasn't as bad as the other outside fears, hence the ability to take walks.

It's amazing that after having postpartum psychosis, I would ever want to be pregnant again. Two years after Theodore was born, life was balancing out and adding one more child to our little family was what I wanted. We had a plan in place to start taking my medication a few days after Franklin was born to help reduce the risk of postpartum psychosis. I was no longer ashamed to bottle feed. I no longer cared if strangers would comment on whether or not I loved my child because I wasn't breastfeeding. My mental health was too important to take a chance on a repeat of postpartum psychosis- and formula is readily available. This isn't one hundred years ago where if you couldn't breast feed one of two things would happen: 1) the need to find a wet nurse was immediate or 2) your baby would die. Thank God for modern formula.

The plan to start my medication as soon as possible work in a fashion. I only developed postpartum mania.

Moderate rant about C-sections. There are some who believe Cesarean sections somehow make me less of a woman because I took the "easy" way out. These people don't understand what the long and painful recovery time is for a C-section. They also don't seem to understand history and the how high the rate of infant mortality was. Or that, dying in childbirth was a leading cause of death in women. That is, until the safe C-section came into play. C-sections save both the lives of baby and mother. Still, you might argue, there are women who could birth their children but instead choose to have their child surgically removed. I say, "who cares?" Babies become adults just fine regardless of how they were brought into this world. Every woman needs to figure out the best birth plan for her. End tangent.

At least with postpartum mania, I spent a lot less money than I did with postpartum psychosis after giving birth to Theodore. Which is when I spent over three thousand dollars a month before medications got my symptoms under control three months later. With Franklin, I only spent half that.

The main issue I had with postpartum mania was grandiose projects that no one cared about.

For example, when Theodore had to spend the night in the hospital because of a bladder infection. I noticed the pediatric wing of the hospital didn't have any children's books for the patients to read. Something had to be done! So I compiled a list of books for the hospital to shelve and instructions on how to do a fundraiser at Barnes and Noble. The poor poor pediatrician looked at me like I had gone mad when I presented my donation folder to him. He sweetly told me he would pass it on to the proper person at the hospital. I'm nearly one hundred percent positive my work made it to someone's garbage can.

A bit more ranting. This time about feeding formula versus breast feeding.

Begin rant: I had to formula feed. I needed to go back on my medication, and thus ending my time breastfeeding. However the stigma of formula feeding is great. I became so tired of being harassed by strangers because of the bottle, I eventually started to make it look like I was breastfeeding.

Avoiding negative comments is something I live for. It makes me change my behavior in public to ward off any individual who feels the need to comment on my life. Actually, I'm not sure if a lot of strangers comment on my behavior or if I over exaggerate the negativity in my head. Yes, actual comments were made by strangers, but one comment can feel like many once I get through thinking about it. I heard more than once that I didn't love my child because I wasn't breastfeeding. It would have been nice to tell them I love my child so much that I fed him formula. A sane mother with a formula fed baby is better than a sick mother who breastfed. Guess what, all formula fed and breastfed babies turn into adults just fine. End rant.

My pregnancy with Franklin sucked. Shortly after finding out the good news, I started having violent morning sickness. I threw up at least five times a day. Which hurt because I was too nauseous to eat anything, and if you ever threw up on an empty stomach then you know that particular brand of fun. Yes, that was a sarcastic statement. It became so bad Theodore would run into the toilet room and pretend to vomit just like mommy. The morning sickness never left me. Then on top of that, at week 23, I started having preterm contractions. I was in and out of the hospital almost every week because of the contractions. At week 34, I got the stomach flu and vomited sitting up in a hospital bed. At 36 weeks, the doctors couldn't stop the contractions and after more than 24 hours of this going on, I was wheeled into the C-section room and Franklin was born.

Jonathan couldn't stay in the hospital with Franklin and me when Franklin was born because someone needed to take care of Theodore and Theodore was unwilling to sleep anywhere but at home. It was just mother and baby. Those moments between a mother and newborn baby are something precious and nothing can take that away. Not even death. I'm grateful Franklin and I got those moments alone because, unbeknownst to me, I was dying.

Chapter Thirteen

Here I Am, Just Like I Said I Would Be

On February 6th, 2016, I walked out of the bathroom after washing my hands because I had just cleaned the kitchen floors, when I suddenly thought, "I'm about to fall." I laid down on the ground and closed my eyes. A rush of sweet warmth flooded over me and I wanted to be swept away. I started to drift into the warmth but then I started to fight. No, I don't want to leave this world. Not yet anyway. The fight became an urgent need. I needed to open my eyes. Open my eyes. Open my eyes. OPEN MY EYES!!!! My eyes slammed open. I did an assessment. My body would not move at all. Not a finger or a toe. No limb. Nothing. Except, maybe, my mouth. Yes, I can talk. "Jonathan!!!" Jonathan came downstairs with my sister and they lifted me up. Slowly I began to be able to move. They helped mo up the stairs so I could rest. While laying down, it happened again. I dreamed during my nap that I died right on the kitchen floor. Warmth ran through me again and I fought as hard as I could to open my eyes. To break free. To regain conciseness. And I did.

Jonathan drove me to the hospital. This would be the second trip to the ER in two weeks.

The first visit was because I started to lose my sight. I freaked out and cancelled the appointment with my doctor for later in the day about my weakening health and went into the ER. The ER doctor said I was having ocular migraines and ordered a CT scan and it came back negative. While waiting for the results she gave me morphine to ease the pain. The morphine didn't help the pain at all. She told me she had no idea why I was having ocular migraines, "Here's some Norco and go home." I saw my doctor a few days later. My blood pressure was through the roof and she was sure I had meningitis.

Let me back up a little. A blood test was done at the beginning of my second pregnancy and the results showed I was no longer immune to Rubella. Somewhere along the way, my childhood vaccine wore off. Whatever happened to the immunity doesn't matter. My obstetrician felt it best to give me the vaccine again after my son was born. I had a serious allergic reaction to the shot. It was the right choice to make. No one could have predicted the reaction that happened. I broke out into hives a few days later and my neck became stiff. I couldn't move my neck which meant I couldn't look at Franklin while I was feeding him. To this day, I feel that Franklin and I missed out on important mother/child bonding time after we got home from the hospital. We would even lose more bonding time because I was in the ICU for a week when he was five weeks old. It took a while for us to gel together but we're there now.

For the five weeks between Franklin's birth and my second trip to the ER, my brain seemed to be losing power. My doctor assumed the Rubella shot had given me meningitis. I had a lot of the symptoms. Pain in my neck and head, a stiff neck, mental confusion, and a fast heart rate are the symptoms I remember the most. Since the doctors thought it was meningitis, rest was what was prescribed. My sister flew down from Washington state to help me with the boys while I slept. Slowly I was losing the ability to focus and not in the normal bipolar way but physically. My eyesight was deteriorating and my hearing was getting worse too. I didn't have the mental capacity to drive and being able to function on any sort of human level felt like a huge challenge. I felt as though I was going to die, but I brushed that thought aside. As run-of-the-mill paranoia. The feeling that I was going to die wasn't anything new.

On that February morning, at the age of 36, I had two transient ischemic attacks (TIAs), or otherwise known as mini-strokes. The ER doctor (who was a different doctor from the "here's some Norco and go home" doctor) ordered an MRI and what they found was crazy nonsense that was about to actually kill me. The doctors estimated that when I walked into the ER I had at best thirty-six hours left to live. The tests showed I had bilateral carotid dissection. (Google says "Carotid dissection is a breakdown of the layers of the carotid artery that causes the wall to tear.") My left carotid artery was torn one hundred percent and an aneurism was forming and my right carotid artery was torn ninety-nine percent. My body had been rerouting the blood vessels in my face to fuel my brain. My face was becoming numb, and not in the schizophrenic way.

Blood thinners were immediately called in and so were the specialist neurosurgeons. I just remember laying in the ER being told I was going to be transferred to the ICU. I couldn't truly comprehend what they were saying. The doctors told me the seriousness of my condition was but all I could think about was how hungry I was. The doctors wouldn't let me eat because at any moment I might have needed to go into surgery.

A top neurosurgeon came to my aid and decided that the best course of action was to let the blood thinners to do their work and I was to have surgery first thing Monday morning (two days after I went into the ER). My sister brought me food. She had to leave the next day and I'm glad I got to see her again, because I honestly wasn't sure if that would be the last time I saw her. We shared a meal together and then she left. We didn't have an end-of-life-conversation. We just assumed I'd be okay, even though it wasn't a sure thing. Then, I was all alone.

That night, I wrote letters to Jonathan, Theodore, and Franklin. I started a Facebook chain to let my friends know what was going on. I wasn't sure what the next day would bring. Life or death. One thing that gave me peace was the fact that at no point did I feel my mother's presence. I have a deep faith that our loved ones who have past will come for us when it's our time to go. I laid on the ICU gurney waiting for her but not once did I feel her energy.

Obviously, I survived the surgery. I now have three stents holding my left carotid artery in place and one stent on my right. The left side stent placement was done two days after my initial TIA. I was given the twilight sedation. Which keeps you half awake during your procedure so you can answer any questions the surgeon may have. Well, I woke up a little and during the whole stent implant procedure I complained I needed to pee. I could hear the nurses calling to have more Twilight given to me. The neurosurgeon agreed to have me put under with anesthesia for the right side stent placement procedure.

Everyday in the ICU, nurses kept coming in my room to tell me how lucky I was to survive. A few even teared up. It took a bit to realize I was a good story in the ICU, a place that sees so much sadness and death. I learned that with my condition half the people who have it have no symptoms at all and the cause of death is discovered on the autopsy table. There I was laying in my hospital bed giving hope to the nurses. I was the mother that lived.

Dad came to visit me for a few days after I got home from the hospital. It was incredibly nice of him to do so. I really needed the help and it was comforting to have him there. I'm not being sarcastic. He took me to the hospital a few days after getting home because I started having painful migraines and I panicked. For some bizarre reason, doctors like to keep this a well guarded secret, but the painful migraines happened because suddenly my brain was receiving all the oxygen it needed and there was a period of adjustment for my brain. I was afraid the painful migraines would last for the rest of my life but they cleared up after five weeks. I can be a little overdramatic at times.

One fun bit about the whole thing was the number of contrast CT scans I needed. I'm allergic to the contrast dye that is used to illuminate the blood vessels for the CT scan and the only way to do the scan was to inject me full of contrast. How was this done since my allergic reaction is to break out into hives and mildly asphyxiate? Let me tell you. I was given Benadryl and... wait for it... a steroid. Yes, steroids that cause my medication to not work. Since it was only a one shot deal and not an over days exposure, the consequences weren't completely terrible. I would just have a mini-episode that would last a few days rather than a few months. The only way to look at it is, it's better to be alive with a small episode than dead. I like being alive.

For a while it had appeared as though my brain was a regression in psychotic symptoms. That soon proved to not be the case. I had postpartum mania and then the voices started up again. Before I knew it, I needed to go back on my medication. The only lasting damage I have from the lack of oxygen to my brain is terrible short term memory.

After getting home and for a year afterwards, I couldn't clean the floors. It filled my heart with terror because the last thing I did before having the first TIA was clean the floors. I would have a minor panic attack every time I saw the vacuum cleaner. It wasn't until I walked into the boys room and found Theodore had dumped baby powder all over the room and was jumping up and down in the crib dusting Franklin with said powder that I was able to move past my phobia. Franklin was laughing incredibly hard. I had a vision of Franklin and Theodore being trouble makers with them egging each other on. Then I realized the only way to clean the baby powder was with the vacuum. I cried but the vacuum cleaner came out. It took me 45 minutes to clean up a 50 sq ft area. It took some more baby steps and frankly the passage of time but the only reason I have for not vacuuming now is that I'm lazy.

There is no known reason as to why what happened happened. The leading theory is that my violent morning sickness caused my arteries to tear. They were clear of plaque buildup, so stenosis was not the cause. Nor is there a genetic issue. Well, not in this case anyway. No one is truly satisfied by the morning sickness explanation but it's the closest thing to an explanation we have.

To top off my near-death experience, I ended up with postpartum mania. My psychiatrist and I decided to try a new drug for people with my condition (schizoaffective disorder with mixed episode being the predominate type of episodes) called Vraylar. The drug worked great for three weeks. Then something strange happened. My thoughts became like liquid. I started to live in a world where during the day, I truly believed Jonathan was dead and during the evening, when he was home, everything was fine. It was a spilt in realities unlike anything I have ever felt. During the day I would house hunt because I no longer wanted to live in a house full of Jonathan memories. I had one thread of a sanity remaining, enough to keep me from hiring a realtor.

After two months the drug's side effects caused stroke-like symptoms and I ended up in the hospital again. My neurologist, after another contrast CT scan came back negative, identified the issue being the Vraylar and not anything neurological. I went off Vraylar and was back again to step one of dealing with postpartum mania. Which like the postpartum psychosis had done, ended with the passage of time.

The neurologist had also told me I needed to lose 100 pounds. My stents wouldn't be able to sustain my current weight and in a few years I'd have serious health problems. Losing 100 pounds is a tall order but I was determined. However, dieting and exercising proved useless because my mind was full of postpartum mania and a drug that was making my mental situation worse. Concentrating on following a diet and working out was too difficult. My general practitioner recommended weight loss surgery so I started 2016 with one life saving surgery and ended the year with another.

I don't have any long term issues from the stroke except short term memory loss. I can ask a person the same question three or four times because I have no recollection of asking the question a few moments before. It's really frustrating. My brain took a physical beating. My poor poor brain. Poor Meaghan.

I'm not afraid of death. I looked Death square in the face, bitch slapped him, and ran towards life screaming "Peace out, sucker!" Yes, yes. That is courageous but I find that I'm deeply upset I'm alive. I am alive out of sheer determination. I'm alive and I get to watch my boys grow up. However, the universe gave me a peaceful out and I didn't take it. I want a peaceful death. How death is going to come for me is a worry of mine. I don't fear death, but I fear how I'm going to die.

Chapter Fourteen

Fun Facts About Being a Mother

I love being a stay at home mother. It isn't without its moments of hell, but I wouldn't want to be doing anything else. There's a certain level of frustration that comes from working fourteen hours a day and being on call the rest of the time. When I'm having a tough mother moment I ask myself, "Is this a mental illness issue or something every mother of young kids faces?" For the most part, it's a mother of young kids issue. I know this because the internet is full of articles written by and for mothers. Needing a break tends to be the biggest need of mothers, but there is no such thing as a break. I can't even use the toilet without little boys following me. I'm surprised I just wrote toilet because I've started to tell the adults in my life that I'm going to use the potty.

I used to firmly believe I wouldn't let my children watch TV until they were two. Hahahaha. Theodore was 10 months old when I gave in and started him on PBS Kids shows. Another lifeline has been YouTube. What in God's name did parents do before YouTube? Oh yeah, stay-at-home mothers became addicted to Valium. There is a lot of crap for children on YouTube but there are also excellent learning videos to be found. Whenever I do need a little sanity break, on goes a video teaching the alphabet. I get to rest and close my eyes. However, dread fills my soul when the cartoon gets to "U." U is near the end of the alphabet thus signaling the end of my break.

Through the years, I have been accused of being an intellectual snob. I'll own up to the fact I believe being knowledgeable and having a love of reading is a valuable trait. However, having kids has diminished my energy to read. I try but I can't seem to read more than a book or two in a year. This lack of energy makes me sad. I try to comfort myself in the fact that I will not always have young kids and soon enough I'll be able to make it through the stack of books I've accumulated. It's a stack that sits there mocking me. Not literally though. Thankfully, those books aren't mocking me in a form of auditory hallucinations. To have the unread books talking to me would be unbearable.

A lot of the strangers who want to talk to me have children of their own. I get it. Parents need to talk to an adult. You know, someone they don't have to use child language for. I spend my days talking to a five-year-old about going to the potty or trying to get him to eat something and he will often resort to Theodorenese after speaking very clearly. I also have a two-year-old who is desperately trying to talk but is still speaking Franklish. A conversation, no matter how brief, with another adult who you can bond with over the challenges of being a parent, is much needed. I don't mind helping the mother out and speaking to her, so I have a little notebook in my head of phrases I can use. For the most part, my go-to phrases do the trick. If the mother/stranger wants a lengthy conversation, it means I actually have to form thoughts into speech. This can make the conversation painful and awkward as small talk is a huge challenge for me.

It is important to make mother friends. It is extremely difficult for me to make friends but it's important to try. I've tried Gymboree, online groups, and story time at the library. It's hard but get yourself out there. Preserve if you can.

At first I would laugh when Theodore had a meltdown in public because anything he did was not as bad as my retail experience. As the years move on and my memory of the bookstore fades, Theodore's meltdowns are no longer funny. Theodore's meltdowns have subsided a great deal but forgetting the trials of customer hell is a problem with my frustration in motherhood. I've moved on from retail into this whole new world of stress. With my book years fading, mommyhood was becoming my center of stress focus. I forgot about the challenges of difficult customers and the act I had to put on everyday. I only had the challenges that were ahead of me.

Another fun part about being a mother is I can use my children as an excuse for not doing things. I believe wholeheartedly this is something every mother does. "Oh I can't go to your party, I can't find a babysitter." Introverts unite under this statement. One excuse I use for not taking a shower is I'm a stay at home mother. Stay at home mothers rarely have the opportunity to bathe. I never took a lot of showers in the first place because on most days I have a fear of flesh eating bugs in the water. That's not normal and something I can't really discuss with most people because of the stigma of mental illness. I can however hide behind my kids. It's great.

My boys are both incredibly rambunctious and it's hard to take them anywhere. I'm fairly sure they scare most people, even those with kids. It makes me want to cry. I'm now the mother of those type of boys. The employees at the local Target all know Theodore. They just laughed and weren't surprised when Theodore set off the fire alarm, knocked over a bottle of wine, and ran down an aisle laughing and screaming with me chasing after him. Franklin is better behaved but he loves seeing his brother be a little out of control and so he laughs. Theodore loves to make Franklin laugh and so he acts out of control. It's a vicious cycle. What to do? Well, Theodore is in school. I save my shopping for when Theodore is in school. Then soon enough, Franklin will be in school and I'll have a vacation at the grocery store.

Their behavior has made my relationships suffer. Not that friends avoid me but last week, my cousin Sean was visiting from New York and we didn't have one of our conversations where we complete each other's half sentences. My boys were out of control. Sean sweetly offered to take the boys to the park for a bit so I could have a break and I told him I just wanted to spend time with him.

The only solace I have is my boys will not be forever young and they will grow up. This situation is temporary.

So far it seems as though I have very few symptoms of my illness when it comes to my children. This is the portrait I want to portray, even if it's not completely accurate. I'm going to guess most mothers don't believe the government puts up surveillance cameras around their house to make sure they're taking care of their children. Whenever I take a moment for myself part of me is worried Child Protective Services will be called and my children will be taken away.

I have no idea why the government occupies such a large place in the mind of a schizophrenic but there you have it. I'm a good mother so there's no reason for my kids to be removed from my house and I know there are no actual cameras watching my every move. But it's hard fighting the paranoia. It's one of my few symptoms that no medication can truly take away. Fight it I do and I shall go on fighting it until either I die or some scientist comes up with a drug to make the paranoia go away.

Fear of the government is a standard issue out-to-get-me paranoia but there's a more severe one: the standard issue everyone-out-to-get-me paranoia. Recently, Theodore and I went to a birthday party for one of his classmates We arrived at the event space and no one was there. After waiting around for ten minutes, I asked an employee where the party was suppose to be. She asked around only to discover the party had been cancelled due to a family emergency. The boy's family didn't have my contact information so we never received a notice it had been cancelled. My paranoia shouldn't have overcome my concern for the family. My thoughts about how the family was doing ran up against my feelings of people out to get me. My thought process looked like this:

"I HOPE THE F t A h M i l s L i Y s I a S ll O a K s A e Y et up."

One interesting bit about being a mother that I think may be solely unique to me or maybe to anyone with an obsession about dying, is I can no longer envision my funeral. I want to when my thoughts are low. It used to bring me such comfort but since I know the pain of losing a mother, I'm uncomfortable with a fantasy that involves my sons grieving. It was difficult moving past one of my comforts when I'm depressed. I know my episodes aren't a tangible depression that can be traced to any one event but I have noticed since the end of my funeral fantasies, my depression episodes are harder to get over. Haha. How's that for an ending to this chapter on motherhood?

Chapter Fifteen

Wait! There's More!

The best way to describe a visual hallucination schizophrenic episode is to say my brain betrays me. In 2017 my brain betrayed me multiple times.

In December of 2016, I had bariatric surgery. I had the gastric sleeve done. What does that mean? In layman's terms, I had my stomach stapled. I've lost a total of 70 pounds because of the surgery. All my doctors are thrilled. It doesn't come without downsides. Because of my stomach size and the need to not eat through my surgery by over eating and stretching my stomach back out and gain all my weight back, I had to learn how to not drown my sorrows in a whole medium pizza, or seven tacos, or candy. Massive amounts of candy. Like candy for dinner sort of amounts of candy. I have found no coping mechanism to take the place of food. Trust me I tried. It's been difficult but I hunkered down and waited out the storm. On the plus side, it's nice to go out in public and not have to worry about strangers looking at me because of my weight.

One of the annoying parts of the surgery is the no drinking alcohol part. For two years my stomach was too small to hold any alcohol. It did need to stretch out just enough to handle a little food with the booze so I wouldn't get really drunk really fast. Sure, my psych meds dictate that I can't drink that much but I could enjoy the occasional beer or glass of wine. It was time to be creative. Over ten years ago, I tried alcohol removed wine and it was nasty. Now the wine makers have found a new way to remove the alcohol without losing too much flavor. If I close my eyes and click my heels three times I can kind of imagine I'm drinking the real deal.

When a nurse asks me if I drink or smoke, I crack a joke about being a goodie two shoes like the Adam Ant song. Don't drink, don't smoke. What do I do? Then I add that I'm a boring person. Though, I would love to drink and smoke on a more regular basis.

There was a time years ago where I would smoke the occasional cigar. It was fun and relaxing. However, after my stroke, cigar smoking became a huge no-no too. I wish I had known that the cigar I smoked the day before my stroke was the last cigar I would ever smoke. Thankfully, I enjoyed every moment of smoking that cigar. It was as if my body knew it would be the last one.

I wish I could say today the stigma of mental illness is gone but alas, it's not. It's a challenge because I recently ran into a mother whom I accidentally alienated at the end of 2016. Right after my bariatric surgery, I had had a play date with this mother and her three boys who I really liked. I made an offhand comment about a fellow mother being snide. (Trust me this mother was snide. I just should have just kept my mouth shut.) Anyway, the one I liked and the snide one talked to each other and there you have it. Twenty-five years after graduating from middle school, I found myself in a situation that could only be concocted by a twelve year old. Instead of talking to me about my comment, the snide one (whose child I shall mention was in Theodore's preschool class) told all the other mothers what I had said and I was shut out of dropping off and picking up conversations. It was terrible but I walked right into it. Okay, I honestly don't know how much of the shut out was because of my snide remark, and their reaction to it or if it had everything to do with the fact that I don't really talk to anyone anyway.

Back to recently (recent being Jan 2018) and my whole point about mental illness stigmas, when I ran into the nice mom. I had heard how tough her 2017 was (which she didn't know I knew) and she shared some of it with me in this brief conversation. She asked me how my 2017 was and I said I had some challenges with my bariatric surgery and ... yep... that was it.). There's no way I was going to bring up my massive schizophrenic episodes. I believe she would have most likely backed away from me in horror. Then she would have told everyone about my mental illness. There it was, I had to choose between looking like nothing bad really ever happens to me or sharing my story. I chose the first option.

In April of 2017, I had my very first full-blown, honest-to-goodness visual hallucinations schizophrenic episode of the year. I started seeing shadows out of the corner of my eyes. Then slowly over the course of a week, the shadows turned into fully formed human beings. It scared the crap out of me because it felt as though I was being followed. Even in my own home. I had to change my medication yet again. I went off Abilify and back onto Saphris. That switch took the shadows away. Great. Then I was diagnosed with cancer.

Okay, it was skin cancer, but the melanoma tumor was largest in size compared to other skin cancers that have a high survival rate. In fact, it was deep enough that I had to have a lymph node removed to check if the cancer had spread. Skin cancer isn't scary unless it spreads into your system. Then it's essentially a death sentence. I was scared. One week after getting the test results, I was in surgery. Everything was fine but I was a ball of tears for one week. It was the most I had cried in a very very long time.

The stage of my tumor had a survival rate of ninety-two percent. Which is great. Mom had a cancer with zero percent survival rate. With ninety-two percent, the odds were in my favor. However, I looked at my boys and suddenly eight percent was too high of a percentage. There was an eight percent chance my skin cancer would kill me. There was a possibility I would still end up as stories to Theodore and Franklin.

What did all that stress do to me? Well, it lead to a schizophrenic episode that made all my other episodes seem cute. In July of 2017, I started feeling the presence of demons around Theodore. I would sit by his side to protect him. I knew full well the demons weren't real but they felt real. Soon enough, I literally started seeing the demons. They looked like black blobby shadow demon thingies. I can't come up with a better description. My doctor took me off Saphris and put me on Fanapt. My third anti-psychotic of the year. Fanapt made thing worse, and shortly after starting to take it, the hallucinations became often and horrific. I saw my dead body hanging from the ceiling. I couldn't walk outside because I would visualize the walk would end in bloody tragedy. In fact I spent most of my days curled up in a ball trying to focus on not hallucinating anything. I'd see my decomposing body lying in bed. I became afraid of my bed. In a few short minutes, I saw my flesh melt off my body. I didn't feel a thing, just saw my skin and muscles waste away until there was only bone left.

One night, I heard noises coming from downstairs. It sounded like a party was going on and everyone was having a good time. I headed downstairs to prove it was only an auditory hallucination but it turned out to be more. There was, in full swing, a speakeasy where my living room should have been. Seriously. There were about 20 people all dressed in 1920s fashion having a good time. I didn't find out if I could join in the fun, I sat down on the stairs and cried instead.

I also had mini-hallucinations. I'd be sitting on the floor and without notice it would feel like I was in quicksand sinking down down down. It was more than a feeling, as the quicksand was visual too. A couple of times I saw rain in my living room. I have a two-story house and the roof is sturdy but there it was, a whole rain storm in my living room. I could smell and feel the rain. It would have been wonderful if the rain was outside and real. All the rationalizing couldn't prevent me from freaking out. I honestly wasn't sure if my sanity would survive. The fact that people with this disorder can fall into the abyss and never return suddenly became a possibility to my reality. I thought I was headed into another life altering episode.

I wanted to check into a mental facility to recover but instead Jonathan took three weeks off from work. I knew firsthand how awful mental institutions were but that's how bad the episode was. I wanted to heal away from home. My four-year-old son was witnessing his mother crying constantly and that needed to end. I just couldn't imagine being away from my boys for any period of time. However, I couldn't take care of myself and I couldn't take care of the boys. Thankfully Theodore started preschool and the time he was in school helped me out greatly. Only having to take care of Franklin was a relief. It was a break from the rigorous task of handling two young children.

The three weeks Jonathan took off still wasn't long enough to see me through to the end of the episode. At least it got me mostly functioning again. Ativan stopped working when it came to my anxiety over my illness. My doctor prescribed Klonopin. Now Klonopin made me feel nice and cozy. It felt like I could take the best nap of my life. However, napping wasn't something I had the luxury of taking, so I became incredibly irritable. Living with the anxiety was my only course of action to give my body time to allow Ativan to work again. The episode finally ended months later when I was put on three anti-psychotics. I'm currently taking Latuda, Saphris, and Abilify, along with my mood stabilizer: Lamictal.

Given the chance, I'm not sure if I would wish away my illness. It sucks but also has made me who I am and I like me. I'm comfortable with myself. Who would I be without it? Would my life be better off or would I discover that I'm completely lazy? I know, I know. Yeah yeah yeah, blah blah blah, you know, whatever. Haha. It's been very hard talking about my disorder as honestly as I have in this book. My illness is what it is. It's me and my illness is part of me for better or worse.

Chapter Sixteen

The Only Person Who Can Call Me a Lunatic Is Me

Some people with normal brains seem to think those with a mental illness are weak. I'll tell you now, that thought is stupid and a bunch of BS. Everyone has their own bucket of shit to deal with in their lives. If you don't think you have a bucket of shit, then that's your bucket of shit. Mine just happens to be serious mental illness and it isn't something that makes me weak. It makes me strong. Stronger than you think. It looks like on paper that I haven't accomplished much in my life. It took me six years to get a two-year college degree, I worked in retail because I couldn't make the film directing thing work, and I have not participated in making the world a better place. It looks as though I'm barely a functioning member of society. My bucket of shit just happens to be an internal fight, one that isn't seen by the outside world. Everyday I'm at war with my brain. Medication helps make it easier to win battles but this war will go on for for the rest of my life. My illness will never get the better of me. I'm stronger than what my paper of accomplishments says. I may not be able to say stress is something I handle well or be capable of working long hours but I live well with a disorder that would make most people weep.

Those who have a mental illness and have committed suicide are not weak. How I get by is by having a personal belief that suicide is the single most selfish thing a person could do to their loved ones. However, I have a lot of sympathy for those who felt their way of winning their battle is to end it all. This is something I have felt a couple of times. One main time was when my first son was born. I looked at him and thought he deserves better than a crazy mother. If I end it all, then Jonathan could find a new better wife and she can raise my son. Then I thought of my mother and all her free spiritedness, and knew I wouldn't change a thing about her. That's how I knew my son (and now sons) would want me to raise them. I may not be perfect but hopefully I can be the perfect mother for them.

There are two parts to every human being. We have souls, the part of us that makes us who we are and we have a brain that makes us feel alive. When your soul and brain are both functioning normally it may be hard to tell where one ends and the other begins. Living with a mental illness, the separation is noticeable. My soul is what makes me me. It's who I am. And my diseased brain is where my schizoaffective comes from. It's not who I am but what I live with. My soul will go to the universe when I die and my brain will be cremated. With death, I will finally be free. If you love someone who lived with a mental illness and has committed suicide, then know they decided to separate their soul from their brain. That's why a lot of people who end their life seem happy at the end. They know soon they'll be free from their brain on a permanent basis.

Aside from my need to battle my illness until the war's natural end, I personally believe (as I need to) that suicide is a selfish act. First I lived for my parents. How could I kill myself? They loved me and deserved to not have a daughter who chose to leave the planet. After meeting Jonathan, I lived for him. It would be unfair to him to fall in love with someone who would leave via death on purpose. Now I live for my sons. I never want them to end up in therapy because their mother left them all alone in this world by taking her own life.

There is a belief that runs through every fiber of my being that there are cameras from the future documenting my life. These cameras are microscopic. They follow me where ever I go. Why they are following me around is a reason only those in the future know. You can't prove they don't exist anymore than I can prove they do.

It's ridiculous that anyone could have such an awful brain and yet, here I am, writing a book on how awful the disease it. Some people have broken bodies, I have a broken brain. I'm not weak, I'm a functioning member of society (for the most part). No one will ever take that away from me. No one but me. However I won't. I love having a life stable enough to have two wonderful boys. I love having a stable enough life to be able to get up and think about taking a shower. I blame being a stay at home mom as the reason I don't shower every day, but truth is no amount of medication can take away my fear of water. Yeah, I know. I just bragged about having a stable enough life to do all these wonderful things but, well medication isn't perfect and some symptoms leak through.

Now, throughout the book I have used the word lunatic to describe myself. Let me state right now, I'm the only one allowed to call me a lunatic. It's my word for myself. Anyone else says it about me and it becomes a derogatory term. I'm not a lunatic to you. To you, I have a mental illness. To me, I'm a lunatic. See the difference? Yes? No? It doesn't matter. As long as you know not to call me a lunatic. Even if you use the word to describe yourself. I will never use the word to describe you.

I have an interesting feature in which I can talk myself out of something I know with lightening speed. Someone could tell me that Lady Jane Grey was queen in 1554 and suddenly, I wouldn't know if that was true or not. (It's not. She was queen in 1553 and executed in 1554.) It's really lame when I'm talking to a person about film and they have a technical question that I know, and I second guess myself. Do I actually know this, or did I imagine the knowledge? Hmm... I really don't know. Then the person walks away and the fog of doubt lifts and I realize what an idiot I just appeared to be. Oh well.

I dislike lose/lose situations, no matter how trivial. Working in retail during the holiday season was terrible and became worse after the whole Merry Christmas/Happy Holidays war began. I always started the season off saying "Happy Holidays" at the end of each customer interaction. Then came the customers who huffily berated me for not saying "Merry Christmas," so I caved and started saying "Merry Christmas." It was then the "Happy Holidays" folks would lay into me. Half way to Christmas I would begin to say my normal "Have a nice day," which it turns out, offends everyone.

The lesson here is if a retail employee wishes you a "Merry Christmas," and you prefer Happy Holidays, smile and say "Thank you." If you're a Merry Christmas sort of person and you get "Happy Holidays," smile and say "Thank you." Most important, if your retail helper says "Have a nice day," smile and say "You too." I can guarantee their work life is stressful and full of misery during this most joyous time of year. There is no good reason to add to that stress/misery by being a jerk.

It was decided when I became pregnant with my first son, it was time to quit the bookstore. Heck, I was even on a hiatus from work for six months. Oh, I know, some people believe a mentally ill person with such a severe disorder shouldn't be allowed to have children. Blah blah blah. People who believe that my fellow mentally ill peers and I shouldn't even have kids, are they themselves probably terrible parents and make them feel better by stating who should and who should not have kids. Stop being so judgmental and live your life.

I don't know if this line of thought is particular to my brain chemistry or if this is a thought most people have. Whenever I am out and about, I don't know if any small action will lead to my death or something positive. Let's say I can't find a parking spot in a parking lot. Will this issue lead me to be safe from the hypothetical bomb that is about to explode killing everyone in the store? Or will it lead me to be in the store just as the bomb goes off? Like I would have survived if I found a parking spot early enough to get me in and out of the store before the bomb goes off. This is a worry of mine almost everyday. What effect will the little actions have?

One game that my friends like to play is if you could live in any time period in history, when would you live? I hate this game because it's only in the past few years that schizophrenic and bipolar medications have been available and actually work. Would I have loved to see Buddy Holly in concert? Sure. Would I have liked to meet Lady Jane Grey? Of course. Have the opportunity to take tea with Jane Austen? Absolutely. However, the cold hard truth is, because of my particular disorder, I would've been in a mental institution. My life is enjoyable and rewarding because I have access to doctors who prescribe medications that treat me. My disorder is manageable, but only in the twenty first century. I completely understand if my life was a literary novel, I'd be the crazy lady in the attic in Jane Eyre. (Haven't read Jane Eyre? What the Hell are you doing reading this? Drop this book now and go read about nineteen-year-old Jane and her love for a man twice her age. I promise, it's worth it.)

Here's another hard fact for me to face. There are a fair number of people who find out about my disorder and treat me like a freak. I've lost friends after I've revealed my illness. It's difficult because my mental illness is not physically noticeable but it's part of me. Once a person learns of my illness, I suddenly become less than human. I become flawed. I become disabled. One of the great things about this time we're living in is the movement to bring those of us with disabilities out of the shadows and to be part of the rest of society. This movement is a blessing. I want to be accepted just as I am. You may see a disability, where I see a human being. Every last one of us with a physical or mental disability are human beings. I want as normal of a life as possible and I don't want to be feared because of what I live with.

I have written, by my calculation, over ten thousand letters. No lie. I started writing letters to a friend, who moved away, when I was in the sixth grade (which means I was eleven. Over two decades of letter writing adds up quickly). As I grew up and as friends came and went, I always looked at moving away from a friend as a chance to gain a pen pal. I'm known for writing letters to friends who live close by too. I love writing letters. It's a way to stay close to a friend when it's not always possible to see them often. I love text messaging because of the way it keeps me close but it hasn't replaced a good old fashion letter.

The vocabulary in my head is better than my written vocabulary, and in turn, my written vocabulary is better than my spoken one. The vocabulary in my head is only better because I'm a terrible speller and my written vocabulary is only better because I tend to have a difficult time pronouncing words. No proofreading is done with my letters. I just write until I'm done writing. This can make my spelling skills cause problems. Fancy sentence writing starts out all well and good, then it all goes straight to poo because I can't figure out how to spell the word or words I want. Sometimes the word I want is so poorly spelled the dictionary can't help me. I could be writing on any subject. Let's take the word existentialism (thank you spell check). The sentence would be all grand in my head but on paper it looks like this: "The movie was full of exsisteilis exitsin exsit (I give up), the movie was wonderful and beautiful."

You might have noticed I spell OK O-K-A-Y. A few picky readers might be getting their grammar panties all bunched up. Hey, I know it's supposed to be OK. I simply don't care. O-K-A-Y looks prettier than O-K and what I think when it comes to my writing is all that matters to me.

I can describe myself using many labels. Mother, sister, wife, daughter, bipolar, short, female, schizophrenic, glasses wearer, stroke survivor, movie lover, bookworm. Here's an exercise: write down all your labels, and be brutally honest, and once you're done, look at the list and promise yourself to be more. Be more than your labels. Be yourself but don't let your labels define you. We are all more than just what's written down on paper. We are individuals, each one different that the other. With that in mind, don't be a stereotypical label.

One last thought before the closing thought of this chapter and book: I take a lot of medication to silence the inanimate objects talking to me. However with modern technology, inanimate objects are actually talking. My phone will tell me a joke if I ask it to. It's unnerving. I shy away from this feature. My car asks me if I want to play the playlist or the artist, when I ask to listen to Nina Nesbitt. As long it doesn't ask me how my day was, I'll be fine. I think. Though I fear the day when cars do just that. Ha ha. Where will I be then? This is coming from a woman whose car told her the car's name was Peggy Sue and they became the best of friends. Hopefully, I'll be on strong enough medication to tell the difference between what's real and what's in my head.

I try to take it one day at a time. I still have manic episodes, I just recently got out of a depressed episode, and every once in a while a flicker of a shadow will run by my peripheral vision. Though a few months ago, I went three whole weeks without a hiccup. It was so divine and lasted long enough for me to believe my medication was working perfectly and I would always be this sane as long as my medication regimen didn't change. I know how my life would be without medication and I'm eternally grateful I live in a time and place where I have the option of medication. I know how my life sounds. It sounds like a challenge. However, through all these challenges, I find I like myself. Nay, love myself. I think I'm a pretty awesome person. This self-love has been one of the reasons I'm still here. Whatever episodes the future may bring, my love of being me will keep me going. So, don't worry about me, I'll be okay. I always am.

All of the Medications I Have Taken

(In Alphabetical Order)

Note: To make it easier, I used the brand name for each medication. However, most of them have a generic name.

Abilify:
Antipsychotic- It can treat schizophrenia, bipolar disorder, depression, and Tourette syndrome.

I'm currently on Abilify. It's one of the three antipsychotics I take. I have been taking this drug on and off for the better part of a decade. A couple of times it was the only antipsychotic I took and it's not completely effective. However, combined with other antipsychotics, it's a miracle worker. It does cause me to have involuntary eye movements. I have to take Cogentin to counteract that side effect. It's the only medication I take that has a side effect medication companion.

Ativan:
Sedative- It can treat seizure disorders, such as epilepsy. It can also be used before surgery and medical procedures to relieve anxiety.

This is my go-to drug for mania. It calms me down quite nicely. It also helps me when I'm have schizophrenic episodes as it takes the edge off of the hallucinations.

Celexa:
Selective Serotonin Reuptake Inhibitor (SSRI)- It can treat depression.

I wasn't on this one for long and that a long time ago. I actually don't remember taking Celexa. The only antidepressant I remember taking is Wellbutrin.

Cogentin:
Anti-Tremor- It can treat Parkinson's disease and side effects of other drugs.

I take this to counteract the side effects of Abilify.

Depakote:
Anticonvulsant- It can treat seizures and bipolar disorder. It can also help prevent migraine headaches.

This is the only medication I remember the first psychiatrist I saw prescribing. The doctor, who put me in the hospital (on my request), prescribed for me. I didn't like it at all. It made me very strung out and I was already unable to function. A medication that makes functionality worse was not good. A few months after starting the medication, I stopped taking it and found a new doctor.

Fanapt:
Antipsychotic- It can treat schizophrenia.

Side effects I experienced: Fast uneven heartbeat, confusion, muscle stiffness, increased hunger, muscle movement I couldn't control, lightheadedness, and dizziness.
I will never take this medication again!

Geodon:
Antipsychotic- It can treat schizophrenia and bipolar disorder.

This was the anti-psychotic I took before taking Abilify. I remember this one well because it made me feel like lightning bolts were going off in my brain. Every time a bolt of lightning went off, a flash of light went past my eyes.

Klonopin:
Sedative- It can treat seizures, panic disorder, and anxiety.

Klonopin was prescribed during my massive schizophrenic episode in mid 2017 when Ativan stopped working as well as it normally does. The medication made me want to take a beautiful wonderful nap but since I have children to take care of, I couldn't nap. The lack of a nap made me incredibly irritable and thus I didn't take any sedative for my hallucinations for a few weeks until Ativan started working again.

Lamictal:
Anticonvulsant- It can treat seizures and bipolar disorder.

Lamictal is the gold standard mood stabilizer for those with bipolar disorder. I have been on it for over a decade. It works for the most part. Mini episodes are less pronounced than they were before I started taking this medication. I believe one day there will be a medication that completely takes away my episodes but Lamictal, for now, offers a life raft for me to cling onto.

Latuda:
Antipsychotic- It can treat schizophrenia.

I started taking Latuda during my bout with postpartum psychosis. It helps with my grand delusions. Since starting Latuda I haven't had a grand delusion. I currently pair Latuda with Abilify and Saphris and these three drugs together make my schizophrenia easier to live with.

Paxil:
Selective Serotonin Reuptake Inhibitor (SSRI)- It can treat depression, anxiety disorders, obsessive-compulsive disorder

This was the first medication I ever tried. I was sixteen and it was the reason I was hesitant to take medication ever again. It made me feel like I was floating and not really alive. It also altered my appearance enough that people thought I was high on illegal drugs.

Prozac:
Selective Serotonin Reuptake Inhibitor (SSRI)- It can treat depression, obsessive-compulsive disorder (OCD), bulimia nervosa, and panic disorder.

I was having a massive depressed episode and went on it in the summer of 2018. It caused my rectum to bleed. That was an embarrassing ER visit.

Risperdal:
Antipsychotic- It can treat schizophrenia and bipolar disorder.

There was a time in 2004 when I wanted to try a different medication other than Abilify to stop my auditory hallucinations. Risperdal increased my appetite so much that I gained fifty pounds. Thirty of which was gained in a six-week period. This medication also gave me involuntary eye movements and I took Cogentin to combat the side effect. After about six months, I went back to Abilify.

Saphris:
Atypical antipsychotic- Treats schizophrenia and acute mania associated with bipolar disorder.

The first time I took Saphris, I had wanted to get away from Abilify because Abilify isn't the most effective antipsychotic on the market and I was looking for something better. Saphris made me feel more balanced, but one of the side effects in women is a stop in ovulation and I was trying to get pregnant for the second time. After my schizophrenic episode in mid-2017, I started taking it again along with Abilify and Latuda. It takes all three medications combined to keep my schizophrenia from running rampant. It also helps work with Lamictal for my manic episodes.

Seroquel:
Antipsychotic- It can treat schizophrenia, bipolar disorder, and depression.

One of the first medications I took after my life-altering episode to help stop the auditory hallucinations. Seroquel made me incredibly sleepy and I slept a lot because of this side effect. It also increased my appetite and helped me gained twenty pounds. I was only on Seroquel for three months.

Straterra:
Cognition-enhancing medication- It can treat ADHD

I took this medication for a few months in 2003 when I was having trouble concentrating because I was so manic. It simply didn't work and I didn't want to try anymore ADHD medications. ADHD is not an issue for me.

Vraylar:
Atypical antipsychotic- Used in the treatment of schizophrenia and bipolar mania.

This drug was made for people with my condition and my doctor and I had high hopes of this wonder drug. It caused me to live in a split reality and then ended I ended up in the ER because it caused stroke like symptoms in that it made me lose all muscle control and I kept collapsing to the floor.

Wellbutrin:
Smoking cessation aid and antidepressant- It can treat depression and help people quit smoking. It can also prevent depression caused by seasonal affective disorder.

I remember taking Wellbutrin during a bad depressed episode. I remember it didn't work that well and the pill was a hard purple shell that tore up my throat every time I took it. I became hesitant to take it every night because of the throat pain and since it didn't really help me, I stopped taking it.

Xanax:
Sedative- It can treat anxiety and panic disorder.

Xanax helped me though an episode I had in 2010 when I decided to go on an alcohol drinking spree in wine country. It takes a while for the medication to take effect and leaves my system soon afterwards. I only used it that one time. Ativan is my go-to sedative.

Zyprexa:
Antipsychotic- It can treat mental disorders, including schizophrenia and bipolar disorder.

It's in my charts but this is another medication I have no memory of taking. It must not have worked as I was only on it for a few months.

Made in the USA
Middletown, DE
08 August 2020